How I got my First Class degree

Second Edition

How I got my First Class degree

The Second Edition of
'How to get a First Class degree'

Edited by
Peter Tolmie

Innovation in
Higher Education Series

Unit for Innovation
in Higher Education
School of Independent Studies
Lonsdale College
Lancaster University
Lancaster LA1 4YN

*First published in 1998 by the Unit for
Innovation in Higher Education, School of
Independent Studies, Lonsdale College
Lancaster University, Lancaster LA1 4YN*

ISBN 1-86220-044-0

PRINTED ON
RECYCLED PAPER

*Cover design by Rowland & Hird, Lancaster
Printed in Great Britain by
Ampersand Print Management Limited
Preston, Lancashire*

Preface by the Series Editor

By the year 2000 Britain will have transformed its elite universities and colleges into a system of mass higher education. With expansion of student numbers and broadening of access it has become increasingly important to understand life at today's universities and colleges, too frequently presented in outdated stereotypes.

So, we are looking for first-hand accounts of experience at the modern university or college of traditional and modern teaching and assessment methods. We would be interested in accounts of all aspects of these institutions such as issues of race, class, age or gender; success and failure; finance; social life and the problems faced by those combining study with jobs and family responsibilities. Appreciation of these issues is crucial not only for students wishing to make the most of their higher education but also for the success of tutors and other staff in providing it.

If you are already – or about to be – involved in higher education in any way, as a student, professor, lecturer, research worker or other staff, we would like to invite you to consider describing and analysing your experience of today's higher education for publication in this series.

John Wakeford

Acknowledgements

We would like to thank *The Times Higher Education Supplement* for their generous and collaborative support. Through their endorsement and support of the IHE Series, we are able to further develop the contributions we are making towards greater understanding of, and improvements to, modern university life.

In particular, we are grateful to Ms Michelle Blore, Marketing Director of *The Times Higher*, for her support of the Series and for her recognition of the significance of these developments.

Sue Weldon
Publications Editor

Books like this don't just happen. Numerous people are involved in putting them together and I'd now like to offer some of those people my particular thanks. First of all there's John Wakeford, the Series Editor, who encouraged me to do it and then smoothed the way towards getting it done. Sue Weldon, the Publications Editor, has lent much needed support and insight. And Linda Cook has helped in more ways than I could easily mention. I would also like to express my gratitude to Kay Roscoe who was willing to talk and to 'Evie' Miloszewska who tried hard to find a way of expressing it all but, regrettably, admitted defeat at the end of the day. A major part of the project was concerned with the passing on of names and the following is a list of just some of those who helped: David Allan who is now at St Andrews; Margaret Evans of Loughborough University; Dr David Langford of Ripon and York St John's; Sean Mooney of Blackpool and Fylde College; Christine Nightingale of Edge Hill College; Andrew Okey from Lancaster University's Student Registry; Paul Rogers of Blackpool and Fylde College; Maureen Skinner of Buckinghamshire College; Alex Thorley of the AIO; and Tom Wakeford of the University of East London. Last of all, but certainly not least, I want to thank Hilary Arksey. She gave me some most valuable advice when I first set out on this project. But, more importantly, it was through her vision and hard work that the First Edition of this book was realised, and without that how could there ever have been a Second?

Peter Tolmie
Editor

Contents

Notes on Contributors

All contributors to this book graduated with First Class degrees during 1997.

Peter Tolmie is a Research Assistant in the Sociology Department at Lancaster University, working on an ESRC *'Virtual Society? Programme'* project entitled 'Where the Virtual Meets the Real: Management, Skill and Innovation in the Virtual Organisation'. Research for this project will form the basis of his PhD, and beyond that he will be looking for further research and lecturing work in academia.

Annie James is presently doing a Masters Degree in *Society, Science and Nature* at Lancaster University. She is looking forward to going on to do a PhD which will focus on 'Pre-Natal Screening for Genetic Disorders' whilst further developing a long-standing interest in research and research methodology.

Chris Waind is a Graphic Designer at Definition Design in London. He is doing multi-media CD-ROM design at the moment and hoping to develop further within that field.

Fenella Cowe is a qualified nurse and midwife and has been working in the field of sexual health and HIV for 6 years. She is currently undertaking a Masters course in Counselling at the Isis Centre in Oxford.

Mark McArdle is doing a Masters Degree in *Information Management* at Lancaster University's Management School before hopefully going on to work in Information Systems.

Kerry Boorman is close to finishing a Masters Degree in *Contemporary Theatre Practice* at Lancaster University. Once this is completed she is hoping to either start up her own theatre company or to work as a Theatre Studies lecturer.

Donna Taylor is just finishing a Teaching Certificate in Adult Education. She is going to begin an MPhil in English Literature in October 1998 and, all being well, a Doctorate the year after. Ultimately she hopes to be a university lecturer.

Mike Barwise is currently working for a PhD in *Digital Signal Processing* at Sheffield Hallam University, but is about to give this up, mainly because he has run out of money. He will then going home to Scotland to finish a few papers and to work as a computing consultant.

Emma Clayton is currently working as a Research Assistant for Warwick University, investigating how pupils with English as an Additional Language are assessed in local primary schools. Her future plans are to further her studies, perhaps to PhD level, and to continue working in linguistics and education.

Dave Bloodworth has recently taken up a post as a senior software engineer, with responsibility for the design and development of real time software under the Windows NT operating system.

Ruth Adams is an Administrator on the Royal Society of Arts flagship project *'Redefining Work'*. She will shortly be returning to university to do the London Consortium's Postgraduate Studies course in *Cultural Studies and Humanities* at Birkbeck College.

Tom Stannard is currently employed as a Quality Assurance Officer at CIPFA (The Chartered Institute of Public Finance and Accountancy) where he is responsible for QA policy development, implementation and monitoring in a specialised higher education field. He will be commencing a Master's degree in Politics and Administration at the University of London in October 1998.

Stephanie Grooms will complete an MSc in Industrial Mathematical Modelling at Loughborough in September and is currently on work placement at the Met Office. After a well-earned rest she is looking forward to a career in mathematics.

Jane Rushton is doing some seminar teaching at the Art Department at Lancaster University. However, she has spent most of the past nine months advising on the design of a visitors' centre for a cheese factory and, with a colleague, painting forty square metres of mural commissioned by the factory owners. She continued to produce her own work and hopes to maintain alongside of this a career in freelance mural painting and design consultancy.

Susan Anderson is collecting sheep droppings. She stresses this is part of her fieldwork as a Research Assistant in the Institute of Environmental and Natural Sciences at Lancaster University where she is currently doing field and laboratory microbiology. She is hoping to get funding to extend her work into a PhD.

Sheila Parnaby is working as a basic grade occupational therapist on a rotational post. This covers physical and mental health clinical work across two NHS trusts in Leeds. She will be looking for a senior post after about 18 months in a clinical speciality, but her first aim is to gain a broad experience on which to base her career.

Marc Dellerba is doing a PhD in Organic Chemistry at Warwick University. Ultimately he is hoping to go on to work in industry.

Stuart Brinkworh has just completed the *Legal Practice Course* at the College of Law in London, and is now working at the New York office of international law firm Allen & Overy while studying for the New York State Bar. Afterwards he intends to specialise in the law of international banking and capital markets.

At the moment **Gary Rigg** is working for the Defence Evaluation and Research Agency. His job title is 'Scientist' and he's part of a research team predominantly producing software. He will shortly be moving to work for Hitachi Europe Ltd as a 'Software Design Engineer'. His current intentions are to build up a good level of Software Engineering experience and then to change the direction of his career slightly by getting involved in Artificial Intelligence R & D.

Paul Sutherland is primarily a poet and runs poetry workshops in York. He is currently doing some part-time teaching in English Studies at the University College of Ripon and York St John and some freelance Teaching English as a Foreign Language. He is also one of the editors of the Yorkshire and Humberside Arts supported magazine *DreamCatcher*. Additionally to all of this he is doing a Masters Degree at Ripon and York St John and hopes to get funding to move to doing this by research at York University, focusing on the work of the Caribbean poet, Derek Woolcott. However, his primary concern at present is as the chair of York Arts Arena, which is an attempt to create an arts organisation with its motto being to "encourage, support and promote the Arts – amateur and professional – in York."

Introduction

Peter Tolmie

Easter vacation. The middle of the night. All of the heaters have gone off. The cold has turned your hands to gelid mattocks that beat senseless gibberish from a computer keyboard. The weight upon your eyelids drags your whole face towards the table so that you only startle back to life as your neck begins to snap. And the dark and the silence are rattling so hard on the windows that you jump at your own reflection.

Then something warm slides into your head.

Some pale worm of inspiration has slithered up your spine to coil itself tightly about your brain-stem. There it suckles on the remnants of your body heat and takes on colour.

For four solid hours you write: breathlessly; the rattle of the keys just a trickling echo of rapid, percussive thought as it leaves your head and paints itself on the screen; the dark and the silence transformed into a buffer that now protects the words as they reverberate through into the early morning light.

Then the first sleepy child staggers through the kitchen door, demands its breakfast, and while you are distracted the worm of a thought slips away.

In this experience there may be something of what it takes to get a First Class degree: long hours of work and frustration; sudden flashes of insight, perhaps, that cannot, WILL not, be refused. But, of course, these are my own reflections. For each of us the perspiration and discovery will take on its own shape, suggest its own metaphor. For me it was a revelatory journey full of conflict. For others it was a business transaction (though demanding long hours of work). And for some, perhaps, it was a treasure hunt. This alone means that a book like this could never hope to be a 'cookbook'. Indeed, the single most noticeable feature of the accounts I have brought together is their sheer variety. It is for that reason that the title of this second edition has been changed from *How to get a first class degree* to *How I got my first class degree.* So I would urge the reader to view this book as a collection of short stories. Not that they are fictions. But in each chapter a different author will tell you something of how it was for them, of the experiences that, for them, made up the story of how they got a First. Along the way they impart advice. Listen to it carefully. Some of it will be for you.

However, whilst all of these experiences were inevitably unique, there are perhaps ways of going about being a First Class student that will leave their trace in any account. There is possibly some sense of order to how a First can be achieved.

So what is a First Class student? What sort of story do the various stories tell? At first sight there is not just difference but open disagreement. For instance, whilst a couple of the writers exhort you to show equal application in all of your courses, others suggest using a far more focused, playing the system kind of approach. And, although a number of the authors feel practising examination answers is essential, another believes this to be a cramp to open thinking. Doubtless there are many other contradictions you will find.

And yet, behind it all, there are certain assumptions that seem to prevail. One of these is the need for the written word. Indeed, one of the things that most struck me about the submissions for this book was their literacy. Even the scientists, renowned for their horror of writing, displayed an excellent command of their language. Chris Waind, a dyslexic, found the writing of his chapter a tremendous ordeal. Yet, upon reading it, I was immediately impressed by the literacy and eloquence of his thoughts. Academia is built upon the written word. Words abound even in scientific journals. No-one paused for a moment to consider the necessity of taking some sort of notes. For those doing the humanities and social sciences the requirement for essays or dissertations was taken to be inevitable. And none of the contributors stopped to question the need for at least some reading as a necessary part of it all. What all of this might amount to is a suggestion that you make good use of your language. It is quite possibly <u>the</u> key resource.

However, I don't mean to suggest by this that those who have long avoided the formal requirements of English courses should suddenly go out and enrol for one because it's the only way they're going to get a First Class degree. Rather, through collating this book I have come to realise that this issue of language comes to considerably more than just grammatical accuracy on the written page. It is about being driven to respond discursively to the tasks you are undertaking; it is about wanting to communicate your feelings and understandings about your work - you need to have the urge to interact with the material you are studying, and with others who are studying it as well. My challenge, if I have one, is to out-and-out silence, to saying the barest minimum about the subject with which you are supposedly engaged. Over half the contributors to this book put communication with tutors up front as one of the most important reasons why they got a First. And several of those who didn't, mentioned discussing things with friends. Learning, it would seem, is promoted through discussion. And that makes me wonder about the possible efficacy of apparently unrelated informal conversations amongst friends in coffee bars or down the pub.

Some of the assumptions people make about what it takes to get a First might be thought of as mundane and rather obvious. Determination, for instance, is expressed as a value, and revision is widely considered to be an inevitable part of doing a degree. Yet it is perfectly possible to encounter people who see commitment as a weakness and who professedly 'never revise'.

To put it plainly, those who get Firsts see coming to university as an achievement - they don't just drift in through an open door - and, having got here, they have certain expectations. They expect to be allowed to build upon that achievement. They expect to be able to choose to do the courses they want to do. Most of them take it for granted that such choices can be made, and they do so with consummate efficiency. And the guiding force behind those choices is, time and again, their interest. They don't allow themselves to be bullied into doing something for which they lack enthusiasm. Having got here they're going to do what they damn well came to do! And, if they are sometimes going to need to grit their teeth in order to do that, and if a part of the deal is that they're going to have to revise, then so be it. When you're keen a bit of hard work is by-the-by (not that it ever really is - remember it's an attitude I'm describing for you here). But, beyond and above all this, they see getting a First as something to aspire to. None of them wonder whether a First might not be worth having, or that they might have been better off without a First.

Everyone in this book got a First. Many of them, for no better reason than accessibility, got their Firsts at Lancaster University. But others were deliberately courted because they did not go to Lancaster and because they did different sorts of degrees. So, whilst some of the contributors could be said to have gone to a traditional university, others went to 'new' universities and university colleges, and their stories reflect a variety of systems as well as a variety of degrees. Some of the authors were younger, but others were more mature. The numbers of male and female writers (if you count my introduction) are the same. There is a broad cross-section of the sciences, the social sciences, and the humanities. However, a number of the authors were doing vocational degrees. Some were possibly in the habit of achieving, but many were clearly not. One of the contributors was doing a part-time degree, another (already mentioned) was dyslexic, yet another had previously gone to university (and dropped out) abroad.

All of this serves to stress once again the measure of diversity. This book isn't somehow representative. In view of all I've said how could it be? And, sadly, there are those who vigorously pursue the goal of getting a First only to fail. There are, after all, a multitude of reasons why that can happen as well. My hope is instead that, through offering a wide range of perspectives, you will find somewhere within these covers a voice that can speak to you personally, fragments of other people's experiences within which you can recognise something of your own, somebody else's story that may play a part in shaping yours into a similar story of success.

But if you don't, then invent your own story. If there's one thing this book should tell you, it's that you might well be one of those people who can get a First Class degree.

"A First? - It must have been the alchemy of the Examinations Board!" (Diary of a First Class Graduate)

Annie James
*First Class Honours in Applied Social Science
and Independent Studies
Lancaster University*

The title of this chapter summarises my initial reaction to gaining a First. In some ways I still don't fully understand just how I got a First - it seems that my time at university was characterised as much by the limitations to effective working I encountered, as the work itself. Consequently, I don't think that this account may be considered as a template for others who aspire to a First. Rather, I hope it will serve as an encouragement to those who have more going on in their lives than meeting essay deadlines.

The First Year

20th October 1994

I have now spent two very busy weeks at university. Unlike many other students, I did not go through the formal channels to enter, and had less than three days following acceptance to prepare myself for the reality of starting university life. I had written directly to the School of Independent Studies with an outline of my main topic areas of interest, namely, women's health and maternity care. It has been fourteen years since I have written an essay or sat an exam, and I have to say that some of the teaching staff here seemed to doubt my ability to maintain the level of academic work required. I must have convinced them! - aided of course by a good reference from my former midwifery college tutor. In the first week here, registration for courses was a confusing affair. I have chosen my courses carefully, ensuring that from the outset there is some coherence between them, and that I am interested enough in the subject areas to remain motivated when I am faced with inevitable difficulties. On the whole, I am expecting university work to be hard, and totally different to any way of working I have ever been used to.

22nd November 1994

More than half way through the first term and I am working very hard. The lectures and seminars are interesting and I try to go to all of them if possible. As soon as I receive each course handbook, I look at the essay titles to find one of interest, and begin reading towards it. It seems as if I am reading ALL of the time! - in bed at night, whilst cooking, in the bath, the launderette, in the car whilst waiting for the children to come out of school. I am using the time between lectures to work in the library at the moment, although I find this quite distracting. I may try an alternative arrangement after the Christmas vacation.

18th December 1994

End of term at last, and all essays handed in on time, though with some difficulty. As I consider myself to be a bit of a dormouse I have found writing at night very difficult, even though this seems to be a very common activity among students. I rarely work after midnight, and find that my most productive time is early in the day.

13th February 1995

Major changes to my home situation are happening at the moment, with the separation of my husband and I. He has remained supportive of my academic endeavours, however, and between us we seem to have managed to avoid upsetting the children too much, which would have meant my feeling unable to continue studying. They have all remained living with me, and their day-to-day routines will hopefully not alter noticeably. I have now set up a part of my bedroom to use as a study area, and find that I can work much more effectively, with frequent breaks for cups of tea or a wander in the garden. As in other areas of my life, I have remained flexible, and really have no set routine for my academic work. I would find a fixed scheme unbearably frustrating to adhere to, simply because the needs of the children have to take precedence, and those needs are often unpredictable. My scheme, if it may be called such, is to work as and when I feel able to, taking into account family needs, and, importantly, my own motivation to work. So far, by working in this way, I have managed to (almost) avoid the frustration of being constantly interrupted whilst on the trail of important new evidence!

20th May 1995

This term, decisions have had to be made about what courses will comprise my degree. Having talked through the possibilities with tutors who know my work I eventually decided upon a combination of five Independent Studies units, and four units in Applied Social Science. With the support of an Independent Studies tutor, I have negotiated a place to do one IS unit via the Summer University, once the first year exams are over. Unlike some students, I know that I will be unable to get a paid job for the summer because all three children will be with me during the school holidays. I also know that, if I can complete a unit over the summer vacation, I will start the second year with one of my degree units done - a head start if you like.

The Second Year

16th November 1995

Despite a good start to my second year work, I am working less and less effectively. I did complete the summer unit, and started the new term quietly confident that I would be able to carry on successfully. However, I am finding that I have even less time available for studying than before, and when I do have time, I am not using it very well. If this continues I will have to see the tutors, a situation I am reluctant to instigate.

20th January 1996

I have finally forced myself to recognise that I am in danger of falling seriously behind with my work, and I am contemplating giving up my studies altogether. I am completing taught courses with some success, but my Independent Studies research dissertations are proving impossible to manage. One in particular has grown to have an identity all of its own and I can hardly bear to look at it any more. I need to move on with it, but instead I spend hours changing the type or formatting - if it does get finished it'll be the prettiest dissertation so far! The pressure of university work, family commitments and financial difficulties has become almost intolerable, and my motivation, a key element of it all, is failing me.

10th May 1996

The last few months have been the most difficult for me yet. From discussions with other students, it appears that many people think that full unit dissertations are an easier option than taught courses with exams to follow. Admittedly, there is no end of year revision to worry about. Neither is there the stress of sitting exams. BUT, I, and others, have found that by becoming so deeply involved in the research for each dissertation, the actual time and effort does outweigh the workload of taught units. However, I wouldn't discourage anyone from using dissertation options for their degrees - quite the opposite. I have found that I am learning much more about the topics by working through them this way. An added advantage, for me, has been the individual support from the supervising tutors for each unit. This has been invaluable, and has certainly contributed to my being able to continue my studies through some difficult times.

20th June 1996

Almost the end of the second year, and I seem to have just about managed to keep up with everything I needed to. I have altered my courses strategy in order to ensure that I can complete my degree. This has meant dropping one of the Independent Studies units, and replacing it with two more half units in Applied Social Science. My degree will still be a combined major, but weighted more in Applied Social Science. I think the exams have gone quite well, and I have abandoned the idea of doing another Summer University unit this year - I intend to try and enjoy a summer off so that I will be refreshed to begin the final year.

The Third Year

14th November 1996

Luckily, my motivation has returned with a vengeance, and I feel able to carry on and finish my degree. During the summer, I didn't entirely abandon academic work, but limited it to some enjoyable fieldwork for my next dissertation and, of course, quite a lot of reading. I think that by now I have a good idea about myself and academic work, and I know that if I can work consistently, I will finish my degree and do quite well.

3rd March 1997

This year seems to be passing in a blur of continual writing and adrenaline. I am working extremely hard although, as always, the time available for work is very much governed by family life. I have lately been considering my likely degree classification. My Independent Studies work will not be marked until late May so I can't make an accurate guess. This does not stop me, however, from jotting down various calculations from time to time. Although this activity is probably a waste of valuable study time, I quite enjoy tormenting myself with the notion that it might be possible for me to get a First if my IS work is to a high enough standard. My experience around the campus has led me to believe that many other final year students also engage in this largely fruitless but somehow exciting hobby!

20th June 1997

I have finally finished all of my degree work, including essays, dissertations and exams. There is a strong feeling of relief that it is all over, but still a nagging fear as I wait for the results. During the last couple of months I have concentrated very much on completing all my written work by the final deadline. This turned out to be a very close call indeed. I was writing up until an hour before all the work had to be handed in for marking, leaving me no time for further editing or additions. Revision for the final exams really only began once all of the writing was done but, of course, because of my IS dissertations, I didn't have many exams to face. Now that it is all over, I think I may have scraped through to a 2:1.

27th June 1997

A First! It must have been the alchemy of the Examinations Board. This has been a complete shock to me. I don't believe that I could have intentionally set out to do so well. I work hard when motivated by interest, and I do think that, along with determination, my motivation has probably been the key to my success.

Degrees, Designs and Dyslexia

Chris Waind
First Class Honours in Graphic Design and Advertising
Buckinghamshire College

The field of Art and Design is open to subjective judgement. It is not a case of learning academic facts that can be classed as 'right' or 'wrong'. Here, then, setting forward a strict formula or strategy to meet the criteria of a First Class degree is a near impossibility and, in my opinion, wrong.

From school I knew I wanted to go on to art college and then into an 'art-related' career. So I didn't have the worries or problems of deciding what I wanted to do in life. And my next step into further education only highlighted what I needed even more: I had to start working towards the creation of my own personal identity and style, whilst producing the quality of work that would enable me to get into a top university of my choice.

Arriving at university, the first term found me starting to drift. It became obvious I had to put my own style 'on hold'. I was expected to follow the exact agenda of the course, which involved working in various mediums and specialisms, none of which, I thought, allowed me to broaden my personal style. From a carefully orchestrated life at college, I was thrown into an environment where I was competing with equally competent students, but left on my own to totally re-develop myself. This re-development can only be described as a 'negative' learning process.

Compounding all this was the fact I was dyslexic. The home environment isn't a good place for learning to cope with it - everyone knows, makes allowances, and shares the burden. It was devastating arriving at university to find people don't give extra consideration, or make allowances, and, more importantly, aren't really concerned about your problem because they don't understand. I had to develop my own strategies for coping. Even though I had 'a Statement of Educational Needs' I found that people's understanding of dyslexia was very limited. One Art

History tutor said "If you're serious about the dyslexia 'thing' - come and see me". This didn't fill me with confidence. Some of the strategies I developed helped me, not only with the written work, but, with my approach to the course. I had to set firm deadlines, with realistic goals, and work within a well-defined structure that had to be adhered to.

The summer vacation was a welcome relief and notable for two things: (1) after working at the till in the local supermarket I couldn't envisage a career in retail; (2) I managed to amass a lot of ideas in my preferred style in preparation for the second year, which began with a rush of creativity and consolidation of the knowledge I'd gained in the first. I'd experimented with advertising and illustration but now I knew I wanted to specialise in graphics and the opportunity to re-introduce my own style and ideas fell into place during that second year. This new found independence had an enormously beneficial effect on my own personal confidence. I executed a lot of new ideas and produced some interesting and encouraging projects, perhaps a little varied in application and approach, but nevertheless self-evidently mine.

The second vacation again found me working at a supermarket. Again there was time to expand my creativity by putting my thoughts and feelings down in various ways in sketchbooks - always a source of reference and inspiration. It might just be the way various colours interacted or a technique I'd experimented with, but it could be the spark I needed to fire an idea for a new project.

It was during the vacation that I started to research and collate my ideas for my thesis. I was determined that before I went back for the final year I would have the 'backbone' of this thesis in place. I aimed to have it ready in its first draft form for Christmas, and to submit it in advance of the February deadline.

When the final year arrived it was time to complete the thesis (not something a dyslexic person particularly desires), come up with major projects, finish work-related assignments, and plan my final year degree show. One of my first major projects had been floating around in my head for some time. It was something close to my heart - dyslexia awareness. It presented me with great problems because I was committed to producing it in my own personal style, to exacting standards, and I would not compromise.

At this time I was approached to submit a design for the University Prospectus. This led into designing the whole brochure, poster, and related work. This 'real-life' project not only gave me vital confidence and experience but also led me into other commercial projects, the biggest of which pushed my creativity to the limit. In a period where time was the crucial factor I was embarking on making an experimental interactive CD-ROM for a major distillery company.

At times it did feel like I had taken on too much. I had very little prior knowledge of how to complete these jobs, but pure determination to succeed drove me on in both my design and my academic studies. Although in retrospect this does sound like a cliché, there is no other way of explaining my attitude towards my work, whether it's applied to an academic or arts-based subject. In completing a degree, you will always deal with confrontations that seem impossible to avoid (such as dyslexia). These problems are often personal conflicts with no way around them. In my experience the only universal solution is to face them with determination and a will to win. For me this was rewarded by being offered a job with a successful design team, and then gaining a First Class Honours in Graphic Design and Advertising.

Having a natural talent wasn't enough to get a good degree: that talent needed expanding and then harnessing to my chosen specialism. Sheer hard work, drive, persistence, and never being afraid to pursue my own goals, no matter what the opposition, gained my First.

NB Clearly Chris found some of the support for his disability less than heartening, something that makes his achievement all the more remarkable. However, readers should note that an ever-growing number of institutions <u>do</u> take dyslexia very seriously and provide considerable support.

Nursing a First

Fenella Cowe
First Class Honours in Nursing Studies
Buckinghamshire College

I have been a Registered General Nurse for over 10 years and decided in my late twenties to undertake a BSc Hons in Nursing. I felt this would allow me both greater insight into the theory underpinning my current practice as a nurse, and enhance my future career prospects within nurse education. Because of this interest in working in teaching it was important for me to get a 'good' degree, as there is considerable competition for these posts. I chose a part-time course (consisting of one day a week formal teaching time), that meant that I could continue my full-time post as a specialist nurse throughout the 3-year programme. Although this retained my financial security it did mean that I had to carefully balance the demands of work and study.

The following chapter aims to share some of my experiences of part-time study as a mature student, and highlight that it is possible to get a First Class degree while both studying and working.

Managing Time

I found that starting working on a piece as soon as the question was provided was essential. I know many of my fellow students tried to complete each piece before moving on to the next. Although this prevents confusion, I found that it was better to do the groundwork for each one early in the term, to allow time for ordered books and articles to filter through. I also found that maximising the time over which ideas on each topic could 'percolate' in my head was central to coming up with interesting or innovative ideas. Having started each piece also provided some (limited!) psychological relief from the sense of being swamped by essays that I didn't yet have the slightest 'grip' on.

Using Learning Resources

Undoubtedly one of the key reasons I obtained a First was access to good library facilities. The eight books allowed by the college wasn't enough to supply all my needs, so I relied heavily on the local College of Nursing and Council libraries for extra books and articles. The College of Nursing library was particularly important as it was open outside working hours and on Saturday mornings. Studying after a day at work, although necessary, tended to produce less effective results, so library visits on Saturday morning became a crucial part of my study routine. Equally important was forming good relationships with supportive library staff, as they gave invaluable advice and helped me seek out and obtain the literature needed for each piece.

The other vital resources contained within the libraries were the computer databases. I found, although reading key texts was necessary, much of the really useful data came from articles and research studies. Searching abstracts provided me with both data to formulate an argument, and material to support an existing idea I was trying to substantiate. Although it was tempting sometimes, when short of time, just to use the abstract, I found the more valuable points were usually contained in the full paper.

Access to a Computer

In the first year of my course I did not have access to a computer at home. I found that I was a poor note-keeper, and struggled to think effectively 'on paper'. By the second year I had a computer at home and found this made an enormous difference. I wrote pieces directly onto the computer which saved time and meant I couldn't 'lose' ideas in the pile of paperwork that was my front room! This facility also meant that I could have slightly longer to work on each piece as I didn't have to allow time for my paper copy to be taken to the typist. Towards the end of the course I managed to borrow a laptop which I took to the library. These sessions with access to books, databases, and my word processor were probably the most productive sessions I spent on the whole course.

Support from Tutors

As I hadn't undertaken any degree level study previously, I took a while to establish what the 'marker' would be looking for. One of the most important things I learnt early on is that it is crucial to work closely with the tutor on each piece you are preparing. The nature of my particular degree meant that the subject matter was immensely diverse, ranging from biochemistry and pharmacology, through the economics of health care and management skills, to the role of the nurse as a counsellor. Different tutors had differing needs and perspectives, and taking the time to 'tune into' their way of thinking seemed time well spent. When starting an essay I would write my plan and take that to the tutor at the next opportunity. Then, throughout writing the piece, I revisited the tutors regularly to ensure that the approach I was taking fitted in with their expectations. This doesn't mean I would 'parrot' a tutor's opinions, but it does mean that I was aware of their views on my work as I went along, and any particular preferences they might have. It is OK to sometimes take a directly contrary stance to your tutors, but you need to be sure you have a solid and well-crafted argument to offer.

It is obviously important to be aware that tutors have to divide their time fairly amongst all the students. However, given the small amount of direct teaching available on part-time courses, maximising opportunities for this one-to-one feedback was important for me.

Essay Structure

Although I didn't use a definite strategy to guide my studying overall, I did have a routine or method for approaching writing each essay.

After doing some preliminary reading I would draw up my plan in the form of a spider diagram. Points that came to mind were copied onto the computer and made into headings. I also, after advice from my sister, wrote the words 'analysis', 'evaluation', and 'synthesis' around the edge of the diagram to remind me to try to perform these tasks in the essay. For me the most helpful article on understanding how to analyse etc was Stephenson (1985)[1]. Although this is quite old now I found it invaluable, and referred to it throughout the three year course.

When writing essays I frequently applied a framework I had learnt while on a presentation skills course. It went something like this: tell them what you are going to tell them (the intro.), tell them what you've come to tell them (the body of the piece), tell them what you've told them (the conclusion), then 'get off' (shut up with no waffling!). Ensuring I had a carefully structured, clear and concise, beginning, middle and end to each piece seemed to be popular with markers.

The introduction needs to be a very unambiguous statement of what is going to come next. I usually took a rather formulaic approach to the content of the first part of the 'body' of the piece, beginning with a number of references relevant to the issue, which helped me to get going. After that I would often give brief historical details concerning the issue in question to provide some context for the reader and then rapidly get on with the key points, arguments or critiques.

I tended to reprise the introduction in the conclusion, and to avoid the temptation to add some new and 'clever' point at the end. I also tried to always finish sharply and clearly, where possible drawing in some 'essence' of the original question to show I had stuck to the point.

It is important to be clear about the marking criteria the tutor will be using. On my course six categories, and your performance in each, were written on the marking sheet returned with your essay. The criteria were as follows: presentation, references,

---

[1] Stephenson P (1985), 'Content of Academic Essays', *Nurse Education Today*, 5(2): 81-7, April

scope of paper, linking of practice and theory, critical and analytical abilities, and innovation. I wrote these on post-it notes and stuck them randomly around the computer screen to serve as a prompt during writing.

In Summary

With both the number of graduates and competition in the job markets growing each year, it may become increasingly valuable to have a good quality degree. There's no doubt that part-time studying is hard work, but it can also be enjoyable and stimulating, as well as enhancing your career prospects. I hope some of my experiences of working and studying may help and encourage you to get the degree you want.

Good Luck!

Managing by Degrees

Mark McArdle
First Class Honours in Management
Lancaster University

First Impressions

"A man who has never gone to school may steal from a freight car; but if he has a university education, he may steal the whole railroad."[2]

Theodore Roosevelt

During Freshers' Week, I remember a PhD explaining the academic effort needed to get a 2:2, a 2:1, and a First. A 2:2 was attainable as long as you didn't get too drunk in the college bars, turned up for most of the lectures and tutorials, and submitted all coursework - eventually. A 2:1 required a better attendance record and more work, but not to the extent that the student felt cut off from civilisation. A First seemed to involve becoming some kind of social outcast. It seemed that students who got Firsts went to every lecture and tutorial (and scribbled notes madly), spent every waking moment immersed in academic books, and were the last to be thrown out of the university library when it was closed at 10.00 p.m. This was apparently vital to the process of getting the 70% plus marks required.

But I am no genius and I wouldn't, and didn't, give up my life for study. I didn't attend every lecture and tutorial. I didn't write down every single word spoken in lectures. I didn't get 70% or more in every essay, project, test, or exam. I was usually behind with my reading and occasionally mystified by the syllabus. Sometimes I couldn't be bothered to go to university and stayed at home instead. But, I always knew where I was, what I had to do, and what not to bother with. And I always worked hard on the things that counted: assessments.

---

[2] Theodore Roosevelt (1858-1919). Quoted in: Bentley, N and Esar, E [ed] (1964), *The Treasury of Humorous Quotations,* J M Dent & Sons Ltd, p 161.

I can explain how I got my First Class degree but I don't necessarily recommend it as good practice. Students must discover their own methods. This is not a guide to getting a First - this is how I got *my* First.

Education or exchange?

> *"Education is an admirable thing, but it is well to remember from time to time that nothing that is worth knowing can be taught."[3]*
>
> **Oscar Wilde**

Getting a degree is about learning, but it isn't just about learning Biology, History, English, or whatever. It's also about understanding what is needed to succeed. That is, what the university wants from you and what you will get in return. You have to get a feel for the education market and really sell your inspirations. What does the lecturer want? What is the essay marker searching for? What is the examiner expecting?

Some students try to offer something that isn't wanted. Others want to give very little - they steal the thoughts of others and submit them as their own. Yet they all want to be rewarded.

Exchange, but don't steal, and they will give you a degree. Think of the university as a customer and give it what it wants. Delight it and that degree will be a First.

Along the way, you may learn something.

Choosing the raw materials

> *"I have never let my schooling interfere with my education."[4]*
>
> **Mark Twain**

---

[3] From *The Critic as Artist, I* in Intentions (1891). Quoted in: *Concise Dictionary of Quotations* (1991), Wm Collins & Co Ltd, p 344.
[4] Mark Twain (1835-1910). Quoted in: Bentley, N and Esar, E [ed] (1964), *The Treasury of Humorous Quotations,* J M Dent & Sons Ltd, p 198.

Courses

Some students select courses that will challenge them or because they think they should be doing them. Initially I did the same and chose badly. I did a marketing course that became tiresome towards the end. It was 80% assessed by exam. My coursework was good, but a poor exam performance dragged the average down. My degree also included some compulsory subjects that I had no real interest in. Most of my 2:1 marks came from these.

Eventually, I decided that if I struggled with a particular topic in a course, or found it distressingly dull, I would simply abandon it. If it became the focus of a tutorial, I would sit quietly at the back of the room. If it appeared on the essay question list, I would move swiftly to the next question. If it appeared on the exam paper, I would cheerfully ignore it. Any attempt to force such unwanted material into my head was an utter waste of time.

So, I dodged very demanding subjects, especially if I wasn't completely in love with them. I favoured subjects that were heavily weighted on coursework and I avoided doing too many half units as they were often part-assessed by exam. One course I did in my final year was assessed solely on a project and I got 98% for it. It's amazing what you can do when you're interested.

It was a major juggling act to get the right mix of courses, but it is really worth the effort to get this right. These courses are the raw materials of your degree. If you choose wisely and get the quality right, you stand a good chance of producing outstanding goods later on.

Books

You could guarantee that every book on a reading list was out on long loan from the university library within 5 seconds of the list being issued. This was worrying at first, but I quickly learned that it was impossible to read all of the books on an average reading list anyway. I sought shortcuts. Collections of selected readings or journal articles were excellent sources that often saved me the bother of reading the original texts. Also, academic books can be difficult to read and understand. If I found myself re-reading sentences or nodding off, I would stop.

Once I started burrowing into books, it was easy to become engulfed in fine detail. References in books dragged me all over the place, but with all the courses I had to do, there wasn't enough time to be led too far. I would flick through the book, read the introduction, note any summaries, look at diagrams, skim the index, and read any conclusions. In all my time at university, I did not read one book from start to finish - I plucked out what was needed and made my escape.

Lectures

> *"Most people tire of a lecture in ten minutes; clever people can do it in five. Sensible people never go to lectures at all."[5]*
>
> ### Stephen Leacock

I knew students who attempted to scribble down every word spoken by the lecturer. I did too at first, but quickly realised when it came to revision that most of my lecture notes were useless. I preferred to write selected notes. Most of all, I would listen. If you are constantly writing, you are not really listening and the essential feel of the subject is lost. Lecturers are imparting their wisdom in exchange for your attention. The least you can do is listen.

Selling the product

Academics as customers

> *"[He] was about to open his lecture, when one of his students rose in his seat and asked a question. It is a practice... which, I need hardly say, we do not*

---

[5] From *My Discovery of England* (1922). Quoted in: Sherrin, N [ed] (1997), *The Oxford Dictionary of Humorous Quotations,* Oxford University Press, p 104.

encourage; the young man, I believe, was a newcomer in the philosophy class.[6]

Stephen Leacock

I identified two types of university academic.

There were those for whom lecturing was an unwelcome interruption to their research work. Tutorials served to compound established wisdom, not to confront it. After all, we were students and what did we know? I would deliberately pitch my essays to these kinds of academics so that my opinions appeared more as evidence that I had read and understood the key contributions to the debate, rather than as an attempt to pull down monuments. I did not want to be marked down for being an upstart.

The other types were those who enjoyed teaching and discussing new ideas. They wanted more. They wanted something different, inspirational, iconoclastic. I would present my arguments to show that I had done my reading and understood the key concepts, but I would also try to add something more to the issue rather than rake over familiar ground. More importantly, I felt safe doing it.

Essentially, it was a case of working out what was wanted and then delivering it. I can't state exactly how successful this tactic was, except to say that I sold more essays than I had returned as faulty.

---

[6] From *Arcadian Adventures with the Idle Rich* (1914). Quoted in: Sherrin, N [ed] (1997), *The Oxford Dictionary of Humorous Quotations*, Oxford University Press, p 103.

Clinching the deal

Exams

"In examinations those who do not wish to know ask questions of those who cannot tell."[7]

Walter Raleigh

My revision consisted of discarding subject areas I could not face revising; reading; compiling notes; and then condensing them onto one or two sheets of A4 for each subject area. Leading up to the exam, I would concentrate on just the condensed notes and rely on my memory to drag out the detail behind them when the time came.

I didn't practice writing exam questions, although it is recommended. I knew the subject areas to be examined, but didn't know what kind of interpretation or analysis was required until I turned over the exam paper. It really is a question of understanding this on the day and I prefer to be spontaneous and open-minded. I don't want pre-formed conclusions filling my mind before I've even read the questions.

The finished product. But what's it worth?

"Gentlemen: I have not had your advantages. What poor education I have received has been gained in the University of Life."[8]

Horatio Bottomley (address to the Oxford Union)

So, I have my degree and it's a First. Does that make me an expert in my field? I remember a man in a pub - a real hard-nosed manager type - berating me for having the temerity to think that by doing a degree in management I would leave university a qualified manager. All I had said was I was doing a

---

[7] From *Laughter from a Cloud* (1923) 'Some Thoughts on Examinations'. Quoted in: Sherrin, N [ed] (1997), *The Oxford Dictionary of Humorous Quotations,* Oxford University Press, p 104.

[8] Speech to the Oxford Union (2 December 1920). Quoted in: Sherrin, N [ed] (1997), *The Oxford Dictionary of Humorous Quotations,* Oxford University Press, p 103.

management degree, not that I was expecting to be made chairman of British Petroleum.

For me it is a symbol of competency and I am *qualified to further my career or studies* in this area. I have some theoretical management knowledge and I have developed some new skills. But, I'm not a management expert.

I've moved on from university now, but there is still more to do. I'm back in the exchange process again.

This time I'm selling my potential for a career.

A Game of Two Halves

Kerry Boorman
First Class Honours in Theatre Studies
Lancaster University

Once upon a time there was a little girl who failed her eleven plus. She went to a big comprehensive school and scored a token number of GCSEs. No-one thought she was particularly clever so, thinking the game was up at the end of the first half, she left. However, back in the changing room her managers encouraged her into a new school kit. The whistle blew for the second half and the game took an extraordinary turn. First of all, scoring enough GCSEs to go into the A-level league, she put twenty-four points on the board - enough to ensure a place at a good club. And then, once upon another time, this same girl graduated with a First Class Honours degree.

So, what happened in the second half? How did I make such a dramatic comeback? Unfortunately I have no secret to tell. My only tactic was that I was willing to try. Actually, I was trying for a 2:1 but, with a First suddenly in sight, my degree gave me 3D perception. That is, my life began to relate to the three dimensions of **D**iscipline, **D**edication, and **D**etermination.

Discipline

The first half of the game had no strategy, no order, no self-control, and insubstantial training. In contrast, the success of the second half depended on active development and rigid adherence to these techniques.

Discipline is not about having your head stuck in a book every second, it's about being organised. Developing a personal training program and sticking to it. Unfortunately, for me this was not the overnight essay, rather it was a slow and painfully paced three to four weeks. I knew if I did not give an essay this time I would either panic or fall behind. Equally, I knew that structure was my weak point so, to compensate, I needed a worthier content, which meant more time, more reading, more effort. Consequently, I often set my own deadlines for about a week earlier than the official ones. This way even when I did miss my goal, I still hit the important one.

However, this didn't mean I had no life. Good time management includes study time, personal time and social time, with the latter two being *as important*. If I trained too much I burnt myself out. Times when I became obsessed with study and sacrificed my social life were unhealthy and ineffective. So discipline a balanced diet.

Dedication

Most games rely on teamwork. In the second half I understood what this meant. 110% dedication to other players, to the game and to myself. This is particularly true when it comes to theatre and performance work.

Firstly: the players. I relied on them and they relied on me. If I offered anything lower than my highest effort I was letting my friends down. The rules are to give as much as you want to receive, in terms of commitment, ideas, effort and support. Whilst pushing others to the limits, I pushed myself and in turn was pushed by them. Tiring. Frustrating. Rewarding.

Secondly: devotion to the game - that is, to the subject and the result. I was never a swot but I always cared about my work. This was the big difference: in the second half I *wanted* to play. I was fascinated by theatre, the theory of its different games and its past players. I believed in it.

Finally: not only did I enjoy the game but, apparently, I was good at it. This I had to see. I wanted Kerry to believe Kerry was good at it so I became faithful to myself and to my potential. I tried to be honest about what I was capable of and would not settle for anything less. I learnt to play better by reading, practising, reading, practising..... I decided when to try something new and when to stick to what would give me the grades and whenever in doubt, to talk to a coach.

Determination

I wanted to win!

Not because I had to but because I wanted to and because I deserved to. I wanted to laugh in the face of the first half. I wanted to prove myself to the critics and I wanted to thank my supporters with ultimate victory.

By setting myself such high expectations I placed myself under tremendous pressure at times and it was important to be aware of potential injury. Nevertheless, I went on assigning myself targets I was determined to hit. My practical work struck Firsts but the mark of a First in an essay was an objective I aimed for for two and a half years. Each time I managed near misses. Until my last two papers. So, if at first you don't succeed, be determined to try until you do.

I put my mind to it and played with unreserved determination. This is the most important factor because such a drive implicitly assumes a commitment to discipline and dedication.

The 3D Game Plan

To be able to say that every piece of work you have done - practical or written - you couldn't have done any better.
I felt I had set myself the unachievable. Against the odds I achieved it.

Can there be a third half?

Euphoria in the First Degree

Donna Taylor
First Class Honours in English
Edge Hill College

It is results day. Three years of working hard - or maybe not hard enough. You swim past people and take a look at the results board, scrutinising the sheets, desperately looking for your name. Then you find it. Third Class or, much worse, complete failure. Your heart beats faster. You are standing there wondering how on earth you are going to tell your parents. A sudden feeling of sickness engulfs you and then...

And then you wake up. Shaken perhaps, even more nervous than before, but thankful that you haven't - as yet - heard news of your certain failure. I had the same dream every night for two weeks before results day. Every time I told my boyfriend about it he just thought that I was barmy. Logic told me that my lowest mark had been 53 so I couldn't possibly have failed. Or could I? Perhaps my final Seamus Heaney essay had been really diabolical, maybe my dissertation on the films of Alfred Hitchcock was so tragically bad that all the tutors I liked and respected were regularly ripping me to shreds over a cup of Espresso. Paranoia set in. Well, not so much 'set in' as took up permanent residence. I was convinced that every time one of my tutors ignored me or failed to look at me when I walked past, it was a sign of their disappointment with my terrible failure.

Ever since the first year fellow classmates had sworn that I'd get a First. Of course I never believed them. You believe that your ability to answer one more question than everybody else doesn't automatically qualify you for 'Mastermind'. All I remembered was my Women's Studies tutor telling me, at the end of the first year, that I'd 'quite comfortably' get a 2:1. A 2:1 was certainly good enough for me. A First was not so much elusive but more a pipe dream. Rather like that ambition you had when you were fifteen to marry Chesney Hawkes - well that was always my ambition!

The point of this incessant chatter is to show you that I wasn't *expecting* a First. I don't think anyone ever does. So here is how results day actually happened.

Unlike my dream, my black jacket didn't whistle or shake as I walked down the corridor. The only thing that was shaking was me. The weight of paranoia was resting quite heavily on my shoulders. I'd had the good sense to go up to college with a couple of friends who, I reasoned, could pick up the pieces should I fall to bits.

We entered the results hall at about midday. There weren't as many people there as I'd anticipated. There I was, alone. Or so it felt. My friend, Peter, had gone to find my results but I think it was Claire who first saw my name under the title of First Class Honours. Seeing my name there in black capital letters made me feel faint. An entire collection of emotions ran through me: surprise, euphoria, excitement. I couldn't believe that I had got a First. In my book Firsts were always for the really bright people and not for the likes of me. Before the surprise could set in and render me too still and helpless, a barrage of former tutors and professors came up to offer me their congratulations. However, to be honest, I wasn't really listening to them. My mind was still rigidly fixed upon those letters.

Later on, when I told my friends that I had got a First, all they could do was stare! Were they staring at my face to see if my (obviously) huge brain was trying to break through my cranium? Or perhaps they were checking to see that my ego was still intact? Actually, it was neither of these. As one of my friends put it, "You must have worked *really* hard, but you don't look tired." They were searching for signs of fatigue! Some great eye baggage just level with my cheekbone that would stand as a testimony to my endless evenings spent frantically poring over textbooks, with perhaps some trace of fountain pen staining my cheek as a reminder of my dissertation.

Actually it's surprising how obtaining a First ignites the jealousy in other people. You will undoubtedly hear cries of "Oh well, she had to work *really* hard" or "she must have worked hard, she didn't get that mark with natural talent". Maybe I did, maybe I didn't. I prefer to think that my degree mark reflects a combination of hard work and talent. To me they are inextricably linked: you can work as hard as you like but, if you do not understand the work, then you are going to get nowhere!

So, what is the secret of obtaining a First? There isn't one. However, if you are following my advice, here is the primary rule. *Do not think that you are aiming for a First.* Set your sights high by all means, but do not start to write every assignment worrying that you have got to get above 70 otherwise your grade will slip. I once found myself worrying about the 'potential' of one of my essays. I'd sit down and re-read it chanting methodically "seventy two, seventy two, you've got to get me seventy two" like some sort of witch doctor. As it happens this assignment got one of my lower marks. All this goes to prove that you cannot hope to wave a magic wand and come out of your graduation day dressed like Batman and waving a First Class Honours. Quite simply, you have to work.

But don't work because you have to. Do it because you want to. If you have a real interest in the subject then you should feel as if you want to know as much about it as possible. If you feel that you don't have that much interest in it then perhaps you shouldn't be studying it anyway. Gaining a degree shouldn't be about how often you can pull the rugby lads or down ten pints - well not entirely anyway! A degree is your way of showing the world and you parents (often the sternest of critics!) that you enjoy that subject, that you are knowledgeable in it, and that you are good at it. It isn't a competition to see if you can get better marks than your brother or a qualification in something obscure (I believe that a degree course in 'The Spice Girls' is now available - need I say more?).

Most importantly, to get a First, or any other mark, don't be complacent. Don't assume that just because you get one high mark for an essay written in a day that you can write every assignment without reading anything.

Well these are *my* 'hints' for obtaining a First. In brief they are: work, plan, research and don't write everything whilst drunk. Enjoy yourself and enjoy your work. A happy student is one who gets the balance right between work and play. Then again, what would I know? I'm obviously an egghead!

Getting a First in Environmental Science and Computing

Mike Barwise
First Class Honours in Combined Sciences
University of East London

There are two issues I would like to present here: my specific circumstances; and the generality of getting First Class Honours as I see it. The distinction is extremely important. It is very tempting to concentrate on the details of one's own experience at the expense of the broader picture, but I believe there is a common (although branching) path to success which is only visible once the detail has been stripped away.

History

I went to university as a mature student, and also somewhat off the cuff. I had lost a job just before clearing came round, so I decided to apply for a degree place rather than remain unemployed. Having studied for a diploma in languages in the mid '70s, and subsequently abandoned an Open University degree course due to lack of funds, I was not in awe of the prospect.

I picked Environmental Science largely because of personal interest. I had previously worked as an engineer on ecological research projects, and I had been interested in environmental issues for nearly 25 years, so it seemed a natural choice. I consciously chose not to apply for an engineering degree, as I wanted to widen my experience base.

In my first year, I did not initially think of specialising in anything of my own choosing. The majority of the units were compulsory, but I did submit a dissertation on climatic modelling, drawing on my computing experience. When this gained a First Class mark it occurred to me that I might as well formalise my computing experience by including it in my degree programme. Fortunately, my department was very accommodating, and allowed me to re-register my degree as

Combined Sciences at the start of my second year. This effectively allowed me free choice of units.

Half way through the first semester of my second year, I went to a postgrad seminar given by one of our lecturers who specialises in palaeobotany (later to become my research supervisor). A chance remark made during that seminar, followed by several hours of intense conversation, yielded a research topic which was to become my major focus for the rest of my degree course: a previously unaddressed aspect of numerical palaeobotany.

So far, my direction was down to pure luck: I had no specific objective in mind other than getting the degree. Neither had I contemplated getting any particular classification, although my marks already averaged a low 2:1 equivalent. Now, it was clear that I had come up with a potentially important research topic, and one that really interested both me and my supervisor. At this point I started consciously to apply a strategy for success. I was not confident of a First, but I was sure that I had a contribution to make to the subject I had picked. It occurred to me that, although work good enough for a First was not guaranteed to be of publishable standard, work which was of publishable standard would be likely to get me a First. My idea was that if I could genuinely produce a professional quality piece of scientific work, the First was probably in the bag.

I was fortunate that my university runs a dual marking scheme: you get the higher result of either the mean of your second and third years (twelve units) or the worst of your best six. I decided to plan for the latter, as it allowed me to de-emphasise some units in favour of others. I concentrated on computer science units and my chosen research topic. My second year dissertation investigated the current wisdom in my chosen field, and in my third year I allocated half my units to a major research project in which I presented my novel work. In the event, I gained a First under both marking schemes (but only just on the mean). I had to some extent misinterpreted the regulations concerning the second scheme, so I did not score as highly as I might on that either.

This history raises a couple of important points. Firstly, *it is very important to have a coherent purpose in your studies.* Enthusiasm for my chosen research project helped a lot to keep me on target. Getting through an apparently random selection of units is much more difficult. Secondly, *check the regulations carefully.* I relied on word of mouth and, as a result, probably threw away between three and five percent (the difference between a First and a good First).

Attitude

Although there was a considerable element of luck in the finding of my research topic, I think the most significant element of my success (such as it was) was not luck but the right attitude. Two aspects of this attitude are simple to explain: first, a real desire to learn; and second, the flexibility to modify methods in the light of results.

In the first case, it has never been sufficient to me to just memorise and regurgitate facts. I have always had a desire to understand processes. My experience as an engineer probably reinforced this, but I remember that even as a child I used to dismantle things to find out how they worked (rather than just smashing things). This habit of mind is worth cultivating. If you don't have a real desire to learn (to know), the degree becomes a mere mastermind contest (in fact: university challenge!) the outcome of which depends on whether the questions asked at exam time coincide with the answers you have memorised. My test of knowing is to apply what you have learned to a new problem. If you can solve it (i.e. you can operate with your knowledge) the knowledge is really yours, and exams become friendly conversations with examiners. Otherwise, you can hardly avoid fear of the unexpected.

The issue of flexibility is at least as important. One will develop a set of tactics for learning a given topic. Some things (for example: terminology) just have to be memorised. Most other things have to be understood. The two will require different tactics. It is crucial, however, to constantly monitor the efficacy of your tactics, and modify them if they are not achieving their objective. Many students of my acquaintance have complained to me that their study methods were not working, but, when offered almost any alternative, presented the stock answer, "Oh, I couldn't do that!" This inflexibility (the fear of trying something unfamiliar, or, worse, the maintenance of a subconscious justification for failure) completely prevents real learning taking place.

It must be said that both these requirements for real learning come down to humility and commitment. I'm not a very humble person in general, but even I can see that if you are learning something, you must respect the teacher's position as someone who knows more than you, or you cannot given them the right kind of attention for learning to take place. I will acknowledge that you sometimes find lecturers (and, indeed, ordinary mortals) who cannot teach, however much you desire it from them, but this does not invalidate the need to approach the learning situation with humility. An extension of this is the need for commitment. By this I do not mean putting in X hours a day, or reading all the set books. I mean the constant recognition that to learn you must put something in rather than trying to take something out. For me this meant spending long hours investigating and reading peripheral material, none of which would directly earn me extra marks. But it was the means by which I accomplished the work that *did* gain the marks.

This attitude of not just doing the minimum is a very difficult concept in our culture, where there is perceived merit in bluffing your way to the top. To really learn, you must give your time, attention and effort. You can sometimes bluff yourself to the top, but, once there, the bluff will be called unless you have the knowledge to bear the responsibilities that come with that position. If you have the knowledge, you don't need the bluff. So yes: you *can* get a First by luck, by memorising, by working the system, but it's a huge gamble. You can almost *assure* a First by thoroughly mastering your subject and applying your knowledge to whatever problems the examiners set you. The First you get by the latter methods will serve you better: it will be a real indication of capacities gained. Ultimately, the bluff-derived

First is useless to you and debases the value of the degree for others to come.

'Treasure Ahoy!':
(How I Got My First in Linguistics)

Emma Clayton
First Class Honours in Linguistics
Lancaster University

Being the first in my family to go to university, I didn't have much of an idea when it came to degrees, including the so-called 'classification scheme'. Even at the start of the third year - informed by my mum - I thought that you only got the 'Honours' bit of a degree if you got a First! Fortunately for me, I somehow learnt more about Firsts and the like. My grades during the first year made me see that I - Miss Average - could actually get a First, and gave me the drive to do just that. Thinking about it now, I realise that I also learnt <u>how</u> to get a First ...

The Treasure Hunt

... At the beginning of my second year I wondered if I was really cut out to do a degree after all, never mind to get a First. The work was harder so my marks plummeted. I sent myself into a frenzy, trying everything I could to improve my grades, from reading study skills books, to seeing the Head of Part Two for a chat - all to no avail.

I didn't know what I was looking for, so I guess I stumbled on it by accident. But I now realise that through a combination of luck and hard work, I discovered what I believe to be some kinds of secrets, or 'keys', to getting a First. My last two years at university were like a treasure hunt, and although I certainly didn't find all the keys, I discovered enough to unlock the treasure chest containing my First ...

... The Keys I Found ...

_   KEY 1:   What tutors want

Some of the lecturers in my department had students' writing as their main research interest, and it was one that I unwittingly used to my advantage. I came across these tutors and their ideas quite by chance through the units I had chosen. Little did I realise that I would stumble on one of the keys when they told the class to: "have confidence to use 'I' and your own 'voice', rather than just the ideas of other authors".

It was only when I started to do this that both my coursework and exam marks began to improve. I'd discovered one of the 'secrets' to academic writing. This, I think, is the key:

> *find out what 'academic writing' means in your department/field.*

_ KEY 2: Theories and more theories

Some of the units I chose presented theories that I found difficult to understand and therefore enjoy, as reflected by my marks. Fortunately, others contained a theory, developed by my department, which I *could* understand and *was* interested in - again, mirrored by my marks. So in the third year, I continued to select units that used some aspect of that particular theory. This allowed me to understand it even more and also to critique it by applying it to my own data, so improving both my coursework and exam marks. It seems that I had discovered yet another key:

> *try to understand at least one theory thoroughly in your field.*

_ KEY 3: I don't understand!

One of the most peculiar keys I found was:

> *even when you don't thoroughly understand a topic, hard work pays off.*

Strangely enough, I got two of my highest marks for essays about topics I didn't thoroughly understand. I didn't really know what I was writing or was meant to write. But I didn't let this put me off. I tried my best and worked my hardest, doing everything that could possibly be required. And somehow, it worked!

_ KEY 4:   Support

At the times when I felt like giving up on trying to get a First I found that the help and advice I got from friends, family and even lecturers was much needed and kept me going. I also found the key:

take the support from friends, family and tutors.

_ KEY 5:   Time-wise, work-wise

At the beginning of the second year I was convinced that you could only get a First if you did as much work as was physically possible in a day. My body soon told me I was wrong! I had discovered the key:

manage your time and workload effectively.

Time-wise, I tried to work the equivalent number of hours to a full-time job - around seven or eight hours a day for five days a week - but I made them flexible by having some mornings, afternoons, or even whole days off. To help, I drew up a schedule for each term containing essay deadlines and dates when I was going to do the various assignments.

Work-wise, rather than attempting to do every piece of work thrown at me, I was selective so that, instead of doing all the readings for each lecture for example, I chose those I was interested in and knew would be useful for essays or exams. And no, I didn't feel guilty.

_ KEY 6:   Dedication

During my time at university I was totally committed to getting a First. Apart from wanting it to improve my job prospects, deep down I was desperate to get it for myself. I also needed a First to make the difficult years spent at university worthwhile. My determination kept me going through these difficult times so one of the keys was:

be committed to your First.

_ KEY 7: Suit yourself

In my department, most units were strictly assessed as 60% exams and 40% coursework. Unfortunately for me, I've always done better in coursework! But I didn't let the system get the better of me. I found the key:

make the system suit you and your needs.

I limited the number of exams I had to do and increased my coursework assessment by choosing to do two dissertations. So as to get good coursework marks I put a lot of time and effort into each assignment, often finding that I only began to understand the essay title when I was half-way through the writing stage.

Where I had to do exams, I just tried to do my best. Knowing that I found it hard to write essays under pressure, I wrote and learnt 'mini-essays', using readings, that I could reproduce in the exams. On the whole this worked. But I still have nightmares about the one exam where I was sat unable to answer the questions!

... And the Keys I Didn't ...

_ KEY 1: Exam time

I found the exams in the third year hard going, mainly because there were so many. Looking back, I think there may have been a key somewhere that would have told me to:

try to do as few exams as possible in the third year.

_ KEY 2: The first year

When I said I didn't know much about degrees, that included dissertations. I wasted valuable time in the summer of my second year frantically searching for clues by reading those study skills books and looking at other dissertations in the library. Hidden somewhere may have been the key:

use the time in the first year wisely, preparing for the coming years.

Treasure Ahoy ...

I've come to realise that Firsts are there for the taking by *anyone* who really wants one. Getting mine wasn't easy. Yet, by finding the keys and using them, I managed to get through the treasure hunt and unlock the chest containing my First. I must admit that I'm ashamed of some of the keys I used. But I hope that by sharing them with you, the treasure will be easier to find ... *TREASURE AHOY!*

Listen to Yourself

Dave Bloodworth
First Class Honours in Computer Engineering
Buckinghamshire College (Degree Awarded by Brunel
University)

People choose to undertake study for a number of reasons and taking on a course at degree level is no mean feat. It requires commitment for not just one term but a significant number of years. Your life will change, you will not have time to do everything and some playtime must be sacrificed in order to work. So, why do it?

Some time ago, when I first entered employment, I attended a company training course, the object of which (I thought) was to introduce new employees to the various product lines and, being an engineering company, the background to those products.

Now the thing I remember most is the chap taking the course asking each of us "why would such a company ever have been formed?" Being extremely naive I suggested that it would have been to satisfy the needs of a market place. This of course was one of many incorrect answers. The only correct answer was "to make a profit".

Such an introduction is intended to put a company and what it expects of you, the new employee, into perspective. You are there to make the company profitable. You should be efficient and, preferably, knowledgeable within your own field. Overall, you must get the job done. The company is investing time and money in you, and it will want to see a (positive) return.

Similarly, in taking a degree - especially a vocationally oriented one - you will be expecting to make a profit. Such a dividend is not considered in monetary terms (not directly anyway) but instead amounts to how saleable you become on the job market, how you are considered for promotion, or maybe both of these.

Your investment is your time, effort and (somebody's) money. The payback is the qualification and this has the additional benefit that you can achieve a higher level of education along the way. Generally it seems that the better the qualification, the better the education.

So, how saleable is that qualification?

As is the case in most other aspects of life, these things are relative. A good qualification has to be better than a poor one. An individual with a First, then, is more attractive to a prospective employer. It says they are good at what they do, they are able to achieve what they set out to do.

So, there you have it. You have decided that you need the qualification and you realise there is no option but to aim high and shoot for the top. So how is it done, how do you achieve gold?

Getting a First does not happen by accident. You have to set out to achieve consistently good results in everything you do. You may hear others say that assignment X does not matter because it does not contribute to the end qualification. It is then that you have to realise that somebody chose to put that assignment into the curriculum for some reason or other. Probably to teach you something that you will need later on.

The rule is: everything is important. Understand a subject once and you will soon pick it up when it comes to revision. You will pass exams because you understand the subject matter, not because you can remember what it was that you were shown.

Now, in order to be consistent in achieving high-end grades, you will need to be committed to your study. You will need to be organised. You will have to plan where you will find the hours necessary to research and complete each task. Also, your plan will have to be conservative because very rarely will you have any time to spare.

Unfortunately, unless you exist in a very tiny and well-defined environment, with absolutely no source of outside interference, the level to which you may commit yourself will also depend very much on other people and circumstances. This is obviously not ideal and, the more others are involved, the less control you have over the situation. A large proportion of those others must buy into your decision to study. If they do not you could well be kidding yourself as to how much time you will be 'allowed' to spend with your books.

I was fortunate. The company for whom I worked sponsored day-release attendance and therefore made their commitment. In addition, on the home front, my wife agreed that she would take on most household chores and allow me some slack on certain DIY tasks, knowing that the course would take some years. Likewise, my son, who was only two and a half at the time I started my final semester, would ask at weekends "is Daddy working today, or can we play?" Even at his age, he could appreciate that 'Daddy' would frequently have to spend a good proportion of weekends in 'his room'.

Commitment is not just on your part, it is required from anybody that can possibly affect your level of determination to succeed.

It may all sound a little bleak but such an undertaking does not necessarily mean years of hard work and drudgery. One surprising aspect of trying your hardest to understand, and consequently do well in most tasks, is the fact that you get hooked on learning, no matter what the subject. This unexpected side effect applies to even those subjects that you "could really do without having to learn". It seems that, as you get down to it, you start to appreciate the finer details and realise that even 'irrelevant' or 'boring' topics can offer degrees of interest.

If you can manage to achieve this state when reading up on your least favourite material, it certainly makes the task easier. It is much easier to find time for a job you want to do! Obviously if you can find all subjects interesting you ought to do well in most. Interest in a project can therefore help to minimise the workload. An obvious tip is then to select, whenever possible, tasks in which you already have some interest.

One of the main things I remember about other students' methods of scheduling and categorising workloads during my course is "if it's worth few or zero marks, it's not important". This approach is patently ridiculous. Which subjects award a lesser proportion to the overall grade? The answer should be obvious: it is those that are generally easier to get a real grasp of, those that you can really understand and use as a firm foundation for developing your knowledge base. Therefore, does it not make sense to dedicate a realistic proportion of time and effort to achieving that higher understanding and consequent higher mark? If you cannot achieve a good grade in the most simple of lectures, what chance will you have later on? Furthermore, even if you did extremely well in a main topic and achieved 90%, this may well only offer a maximum of 18% (from 20) to the overall grade. In that case, unless you have achieved good marks in your other subjects, you can wave goodbye to your First.

Weighting of subject marks is of no consequence, you have to do well across the board.

The solution, then, is to work at the 'all important average'. Do well in the relatively easy subjects early on in the course and this will pump up your average mark. You will find that as you progress into the core material, and the going gets a little harder, the habit of achieving will stick. This average is your buffer between doing very well and just doing well. If you can build it up from the start of the course it is much easier to come to terms with those inevitable lower marks that will dent it every so often. While on the subject of lesser marks, it pays to have some form of plan for coping with them. Never just write them off as a bad experience. You ought to find out what actually went wrong.

Planning or scheduling is really the answer to most aspects of studying. Do not leave anything to chance. Again, even this will become habitual in the end. In any area, it is always difficult to get started and a plan is a good way of focusing the mind. The sooner you work out what you need to do and when you need to have it completed, the simpler the whole task will become. The first off the mark is more likely to be successful because such a technique allows the maximum time possible for thinking over the problem.

Thinking time is not only important at the front end of a project but at the back end too. Once you have completed a task you will know more about it than you could possibly have known beforehand. Does it not then, make sense to allow time to use that knowledge for critically reviewing what it is that you have produced? This time is invaluable. It will allow the opportunity to tune the piece of work until it is consistent with the standard that you will have come to expect of yourself. Sometimes it is only the fact that you know you can do better that will drive you on to putting in the extra effort.

Listen to yourself. Put in that effort and come out on top.

Advice for First Class Wannabes from Swotty Spice

Ruth Adams
First Class Honours in Sociology and Visual Culture
Lancaster University

To get a First you have to be a Spice Girl. By this I don't mean that you need to flash your knickers or get your tongue pierced (although university is probably the only place in your adult life where you won't get judged on your appearance by those in authority - so go for it!). No, what I mean is that to get a First it has to be what you want, what you really, really want. You will do well at university if you have made a conscious decision that studying is what you would rather be doing than anything else for the three years you are there, instead of just ending up there because that's what everybody else does after their A-levels or you don't fancy a job. This, perhaps, explains why mature students often fare better. I went to university after five years in the workplace, and not only had I got most of the usual fresher pre-occupations - losing my virginity, getting blasted on cheap booze, coping without Mum doing the cooking, washing etc - out of the way, I also had no doubt that studying would be, for me, a luxury rather than a chore.

While I've little doubt that it would be possible to achieve a First, given sufficient brains and application, in a discipline in which you had little interest, it would be a very long, hard slog and it would seem senseless to willingly submit to such a lengthy torture. So, as far as I'm concerned, the most crucial element in doing well academically is to *enjoy your subject.*

A good start towards getting a First is to go to as many lectures and seminars as possible. Students often don't attend, perhaps because they are struggling to meet coursework deadlines or, more usually, because they had one too many the night before, but this is a mistake. Having a full set of lecture notes is invaluable when exam time comes around. In addition, being a regular attendee can have spin-off benefits. It would be quite wrong of me to suggest that you will endear yourself to your tutor so much that they will bump up your essay marks a little, but where it can help is if you hit a rocky patch, medical, emotional, academic, or whatever. If you are known as a keen and dedicated student you don't run the risk of being dismissed as a slacker with a sob story. Attending lectures and seminars is also useful as they offer an opportunity to ask questions or clear up points you are not sure about. If in doubt about anything - *ask*! It will not make you look stupid, just interested. You will also probably be doing the rest of the class a favour, as most of them were probably pondering the same 'stupid' question too.

Showing enthusiasm and fostering good relations with staff has all manner of benefits. In my experience really keen students are fairly thin on the ground, so your tutor will probably see you as a blessing rather than a curse and be only too eager to offer extra help, advice and information. And good student/staff relationships can be useful beyond graduation. Remember, it may be that your academic references determine whether you succeed in getting your dream job or postgraduate place and funding.

As I have suggested, if you *are* interested in your subject it makes all of the extra effort you need to put in to get a First so much easier. While the information given by teaching staff in lectures and seminars is extremely valuable, it's not enough on its own - regard it as a jumping off point for your own reading and research. Getting First Class marks requires additional effort and understanding and a demonstration of original, or at least first-hand, thought on a topic.

Read up on your subject in your spare time as much as you can. This reading doesn't have to be directly related to your course topics, in some ways it's better if it's not. Pick related topics that you have a particular interest in. This will allow some respite from the demands of the course whilst gradually building up a broader picture and understanding of your discipline. I found it useful to keep a scrapbook of relevant articles from newspapers and magazines that provided additional source material for essay writing.

Exams. Everyone has their own approach to exams, but here are a few pointers that worked for me. If you can, avoid sitting all your exams in your final year. Spreading exams means that you don't have such a huge and daunting prospect at the end of it all. Furthermore, it's (perhaps not) amazing how much you can forget in a year. When studying for exams for courses you took some time ago you may find that you have to re-learn as well as re-vise, doubling your workload. Exam study requires, I find, almost exactly the opposite approach to coursework. You do not need additional information outside the course boundaries - in fact it's probably a good idea to avoid it as sometimes it can confuse and frustrate a tired and stressed-out mind. Examiners are not looking for evidence of original thought. All they really want to know is whether you have understood, and can recount, the course material effectively. When picking revision topics, I tend to go for those that I am fairly familiar with and which are not too nebulous. Be careful that you don't get complacent about revising for those courses and topics that you feel you are good at or know well. My exam results were worst for my two 'best' courses for that very reason.

Generally speaking, the keys to a First are self-discipline, self-motivation and pride in your work. Although impending deadlines can enforce the odd compromise, try never to hand in a piece of work that isn't the very best that you could do. Always strive for a higher mark next time, even if the previous ones were good. Keep trying to push yourself that little bit further. However, as I have already emphasised, doing a degree should be fun. All students, no matter how bright and dedicated they are, have times when they really can't face opening another book or writing another word. Take the day or the night off, relax and do something unrelated to your studies. Give your brain a rest.

I can't emphasise enough how important it is to maintain an active social and private life - after all, better to be an interesting and sociable person with a First than a boring hermit with one. However, I found that the best thing to do was to separate the two as much as possible. There's absolutely no point in going down the pub and then trying to finish off an essay afterwards. Your night out will be impaired by the knowledge of what's waiting for you at home and your work probably won't be much cop either. Give your academic life and your social life your all, just don't try to do it simultaneously!

Good luck and *have fun*!

First Impressions:
Letter From a Recent Graduate

Tom Stannard
First Class Honours in Politics
Lancaster University

Dear Cathy

There's never an easy way to give straightforward advice to an undergraduate friend in a letter like this. For starters, the fact that you're not reading the same subject that I did, or doing so at the same university, makes giving you focused advice a bit of a problem. But I do think that there are certain things I can tell you which may be of help if, as you say, you're aiming for a First Class degree. I'll start with something fairly personal and then move on to something more general that might interest you a bit more!

What happened to me

When I came to choose my courses I was always conscious of the fact that in such a broad discipline, I shouldn't close off different options from the outset. Had I registered for Politics and International Relations, for example, I would have committed myself to reading a certain number of IR courses during my degree. Not doing so ensured that, although I did have specialised research interests, I could still take some pretty diverse courses. This meant that the degree retained a 'freshness' that contributed to its holding my interest.

It's important to try to maintain a healthy interest in, and enthusiasm for, your subject whilst you're studying it. In my case, following current affairs helped with contemporary government courses, and devoting a lot of time to reading helped a lot with others. If you select your courses carefully and take those that you're actually interested in, this shouldn't prove to be too much of an ordeal. On Arts courses it's particularly important to develop your own methods for tackling the overwhelming amount of reading you're expected to cover. I found personally that I could cope with long periods in front of books, but it often helps to break it up.

I also found it was important to concentrate a lot on coursework. You need to do as well as you can in it if you're going to hit the top grades. The way I approached mine was to work out some kind of timetable for each piece of work I was given. Most of my courses allowed for this by giving the deadlines for essays at the start of the course. I got a year planner and put all the deadlines on it so that I could see exactly how much time I could allow for each. After doing a few essays I found that my working speed allowed me to give at least a week to an average 2-3,000 word essay. I spent most of this time reading, note-taking and planning. I also found it very helpful to allow a decent amount of time to just sit and think about the topic in question - usually after I'd read all the relevant texts, but before I started writing. A decent essay always made me feel really good (above all, really *motivated*), and if you can get a high average on your coursework it's always a good base for your exams. A word on written work here. Sometimes my tutors gave out written work to make us do 'that little bit extra'. These often took the form of book reports, reviews and so on and were frequently *unassessed*. If you find that the same happens on your course, don't waste your time on them. It's beyond me why university tutors hand out tasks like this but you shouldn't allow them to make you neglect your assessed work. Focusing on what you will actually get *marks* for should always be your priority.

You should also make the most of your tutors. It's no joke that the days of regular contact hours with university tutors are numbered. Fairly soon, with the vast increase in the numbers of students going into higher education, English universities will move even further towards a system of lecturing to very large audiences and offering little or no contact hours with undergraduates. I always found it worthwhile to let my tutors know how I was getting on, and to ask for help if I needed it. Most tutors were surprisingly forthcoming as long as I made the first move. It's likely to make the whole degree easier if you make sure you show your tutors that you're interested and prepared to go to them if necessary. It also helps to establish decent professional relationships with them which helps when they come to write your references!

What could happen to you (or anyone!)

I don't think it's unfair to say that everyone's capable of getting a First Class degree. Everyone has different approaches and reactions to what they study, of course, but most people like you who want to get a First and think they're capable of doing so will be disheartened if they don't. However, remember that we don't mark our own exam scripts (much as we'd like to), and personally if I'd graduated with a 2:1 or a 2:2 it wouldn't have been by any means a 'bad' degree and I'd undoubtedly have still valued it as a formidable achievement in itself.

Returning to coursework, different courses give different weight to coursework and you need to draw a careful balance. Needless to say don't spend a day on an essay worth 70% of a course and then do 3 months' revision for the exam. But remember your coursework average doesn't predetermine your final degree classification. My own coursework average was a solid to high 2:1 and I thought that settled the outcome. But, as I found out, sufficient revision for the exams brought it up to a First.

With exams themselves the same points about structured or timetabled work apply. Even when you're better at one course than another remember you're going to be assessed across *all of them,* so don't prioritise revision. Also, make sure that you're well covered. If a paper wants three essays be sure to revise at least five topics. For one of my final papers I was originally going to revise just three topics and then upped it to five. This was the right move as in the end my original three topics all appeared in the first question and in no other! I also made sure that I read past papers that turned out to be a great help. And when I was in the second year I deliberately got to know a few finalists who offered me 'specialist' advice on certain courses (and occasionally on the harshness or leniency of certain markers).

But the best advice I could offer you as a prospective finalist is not to panic. I know this is easier said than done but remember that as you were bright enough to get into university, clearly you're bright enough to do well at university. If you plan your work so that you perform solidly in coursework and do the same with your revision, there's every chance you'll be able to stamp out your nerves by saying to yourself over and over again "I know this stuff, and I *will* do well".

Before I finish, a couple of points about you as a person, and your prospects. Your prospects will certainly be enhanced if you do get a First Class degree. However, this doesn't mean that jobs will fall into your lap as soon as you graduate. A First is a prestigious qualification that's definitely worth having, particularly if you intend to go on and do further research in your field (as you hinted you would at one point). But you must always remember that prospective employers will be interested as much, if not more, in who you are as a person as they will be in what your degree certificate says about you. You should always bear in mind that staying in all the time and literally burying yourself in academic work is *not* the best way to get a good result. I know you don't need to be told about how to enjoy yourself, but just make sure that you do. It's possible to go to a good university and get the most out of it both academically *and* socially. Though some might not believe it if you told them, I graduated with a lot of good friends, a sizeable overdraft, loans, experience of too many good nights out, a taste for quality relationships with other people *and* a First Class degree. It can be done. The rest, as they say, is up to you.

Good Luck, and stay in touch,

Tom

Making the Most of Maths

Stephanie Grooms
First Class Honours in Mathematics
Lancaster University

Earlier this year I graduated with a First Class degree in mathematics. I realised very early on in my degree that I wanted a First but at the end of my second year I was only a borderline candidate for achieving one, so my only hope of fulfilling my aim was to start working seriously hard. I wanted my First badly, so this was my course of action.

Why do you want your First?

Around the middle of my final year I decided that I wanted to continue studying after I'd completed my first degree. Upon doing some investigation in the areas I wished to pursue I became aware that, if I wanted to do that, I needed a good degree to finance both the course and myself through doing it (I have no wish that my parents should support me forever - in fact they have the same wish!). I believe this need for a First made me more willing to put in the hours of work that I needed to do. I could see what having a First would mean to my life after my degree had finished. So, what would a First mean to *you*? And where would it take you in *your* life?

My learning practices

Everybody has their own way of learning and the following is just the way that I worked whilst at Lancaster. I don't know about other degrees but maths has a very structured way in which it is taught. I generally attended all my lectures and if I ever missed any I would always copy up the notes ASAP. I found that by attending lectures I would absorb the information taught far more easily than if I just copied it up later.

My maths courses were organised in such a way that I would usually have to hand in a piece of work each week for them. I found this was very helpful because it made me sit down and read through the work learnt during the week. I would often get stuck attempting to do the questions and in these circumstances I would either go to the library or try and find my friends to see if they had answered them. Asking friends for help was a lot easier than asking the lecturer, and my friends would generally give a totally different way of looking at a problem. This often solved some of the confusion I had about the topic in hand. At the same time I was often asked for help. I found this advantageous as it made me think about how I understood the topic and how I could explain it to someone else, thus improving my own grasp of it.

Choosing courses

When choosing my options for my third year I specifically chose courses that I knew I liked. In maths at Lancaster you can choose from courses on the pure side or the statistics side. My strengths were on the pure side and, as I knew this, I deliberately took all pure courses except for one. This was a maths in education course, taken for the specific reason that it was entirely coursework based. I preferred such courses because they cut down on the number of exams that I had to sit. Also, when exam time came round, it meant that I went into my exams knowing that I had already completed a substantial part of my degree and that lessened the pressure. Which leads me to......

The exams themselves

As these were the most important exams in my life so far I decided that I would try to do as much revision as possible. In the end it worked out that I revised for about eight weeks in total. My first plan of action was to decide how to divide up my time so that I used it as effectively as I could. I drew up a timetable to cover up until the first lot of exams started. After completing those I devised a new, weekly timetable so that I could give more time to the areas I felt needed further work. I divided my day into three to cover the morning, the afternoon and the evening. Into each slot I inserted a subject I wanted to cover during that time. I generally gave myself the evenings off during the beginning of the revision period - unless I had been busy doing other things like shopping during the day! I tried not to give myself a day off as I felt it was important to get into a rhythm whereby I would spend at least four to five hours each day studying. I also tried to start revising from about nine o'clock each morning as this was the time that I would be doing morning exams. This got me and my brain into the habit of being awake at that time of the morning. And the closer the exams came the more revision I would do each day.

I started my revision for a course by going through all my notes and rewriting the bits and proofs that I knew were examinable. Where I had to learn longer proofs or methods for solving problems I would split the proof or method into smaller sections and then try and learn the sections individually. I aimed to look at each course in depth to begin with so as to try and absorb as much information as possible. Then, when I returned to revise that course, I would build upon what I already knew. I would always write down stuff whilst revising, even if I ended up copying the page word for word. This helped me to memorise information that I needed to know off by heart. Maths tends to have a large bookwork component in its exams. By this I mean questions in exams which say "state the such 'n' such law" and so forth. Questions like this cannot be attempted unless the answer is already known. And one isn't going to know it unless it has been learnt thoroughly. It also helps to look through and have a go at old exam papers. These gave me some idea about the type of questions to expect and how the questions were structured. Any time I found questions I couldn't do or proofs I didn't understand I would write them down and then go and find my tutor to explain them. I found this very helpful, especially when he went through exam questions with me. He also explained what the examiner was looking for with certain types of questions, and how much of an answer was expected.

I would generally revise for the length of a CD (or about an hour and a bit) before taking a fifteen minute coffee break (whenever I revise I'm on about ten cups of coffee a day, so, for me, good coffee is a must!). I found revising to a CD advantageous because it was an ideal length of time. I would also plan my lunch and dinner breaks so that they coincided with programmes to watch on telly. This gave me something to look forward to (admittedly the storylines in *Home and Away* or *Neighbours* aren't much to look forward to, but it was enough). I extended this theme by occasionally planning treats in the evening, such as going to the cinema, as a reward to myself for a good day's revision.

A final word

University is much more than a place to study. It is unlikely that after university you will ever encounter another situation that provides such an opportunity to experience so much. So make the most of it.

When the Going Gets Tough...
For A.F.R. 1921-1997

Jane Rushton
First Class Honours in Visual Culture
Lancaster University

When I made the decision to improve my education at the age of thirty-eight, it was because I felt it was severely lacking. What I now see as a series of unfortunate events from the age of eleven had meant that I had never even started to fulfil the potential that I secretly believed I had. I wanted to prove something both to myself and to those who I felt had doubted me. I had been working at the university for ten years as a drawing office technician, had seen students come and go, been an observer of their struggles and their achievements, when I realised that I wanted to make up for opportunities lost and become a student too.

With entry requirements for university successfully achieved (a miracle in itself, I thought), I embarked on the new degree scheme of Visual Culture within the Art Department. This area, I felt, would broaden and deepen my framework of knowledge about art, the practice of which has always been a central part of my life.

How did I get a First in Visual Culture? I don't know, perhaps they made a mistake! While in the first year I might have harboured vague dreams of getting a First, but these dreams soon disappeared. At the beginning of Part Two I had to rethink my priorities and establish a new routine which would allow me to be the support I wanted to be for my father who was diagnosed as having cancer, as well as continuing to be a dedicated partner, mother and student. From this point on my university experience changed. In one sense success became even more important, not in terms of getting a First, but in terms of completing the course moderately well given difficult circumstances. I became desperate not to lose this opportunity which I had waited for for so long.

Getting a First Class degree has, I believe, an awful lot to do with chance - not luck, but chance. The sort of chance that dictates whether or not a partner will ultimately be supportive and not resentful of the time devoted to work (I know of several mature women students who have had that experience); whether courses on offer live up to expectations; whether staff are inspiring and approachable; and, last but not least, whether your hoped-for questions come up on the exam papers. Having identified the role of chance in all this, it has to be said that there are several things a student can do to optimise those chances with the aim of getting a good degree. I've described these under the headings of *Attitude*, *Organisation*, and *Exams, Revision and Technique*.

Attitude

In order to do well you must first *want* to do well, and be prepared to put in a lot of effort. It seems to me that the university experience must be more fulfilling if you are interested and involved in your work. From a very early stage I realised that the system is 'user friendly', but more so if you are a 'friendly user': that is, if you learn how to play it. Help, assistance and guidance are always available, but it's no good expecting it all to be handed to you on a plate - you want it ... you ask for it. I always found that rather than being seen as a nuisance, my questions were welcomed and time was freely given. I can only imagine that by showing an interest I was appealing to these people's passion for their subject.

Organisation

As a mature student with complicated family commitments, I never put off until tomorrow what I could do today, for the simple reason that I never knew what else tomorrow would throw at me. I believe that my managing to stay 'on top' was mainly the result of being highly organised, made easier by having a partner who was prepared to take over many home responsibilities, so that it was possible for me to study when I needed to.

The system in the Art Department requires that students do 'set readings' prior to each lecture, and that they answer a series of questions from reading guidance sheets. These reading notes are handed in with essays and provide additional evidence of understanding. They were often enormously time-consuming but their value was to be appreciated a second time round when it came to exam revision. The moral of this is that only through doing what has been asked of you to the best of your ability can you expect the rewards of knowledge.

Deciding the structure of your degree, i.e. which courses you take, also falls under this heading. Knowing yourself, your strengths and weaknesses is valuable when deciding on a strategy for success. Having always considered that my main weakness was exams I chose my courses specifically to allow for the greatest number of 100% coursework assessments. This meant that a lot of the work was unstructured and self-driven: I would identify topics and research areas and basically get on with it. That way I could tailor projects to my interests and abilities and give myself a better chance of doing good work. Another advantage was that I could then organise my work routine to suit myself without the constraints of an imposed timetable. For example, I could take advantage of the fact that the early morning hours have always been my most productive, while the rest of the world is still asleep. I could get the equivalent of half a day's work over by the time most of my fellow students were stirring from their slumbers.

Exams, Revision and Technique

Despite my having completed five units out of the necessary nine as 100% coursework assessed, I was still faced with five formal examinations in the final year. Unfortunate timing of deadlines for the major dissertation and unreasonable workload requirements meant that it felt as though there was insufficient time for decent revision. So, having sorted out a revision timetable that made sensible use of the remaining time, it was essential to stick to it rigidly. Even though it sometimes felt as though I hadn't covered enough ground in a subject, when the time was up I moved on.

Revision meant reading the relevant set readings, lecture notes and reading notes which had been identified either through revision seminars, revision guidance sheets or through listening carefully to the 'messages' a lecturer was passing. Past papers proved invaluable in giving insight into the sort of emphasis which might appear within a question, though I did not spend too much time writing out full answers to past papers as they were unlikely to appear in my exams. Revision continued up to and throughout the exam period and, although I felt under pressure, I also felt that things were under control.

By the time the exams came I felt that my fate was probably already sealed: at least that, as long as I didn't do anything totally stupid and given a good following wind, I could get a 2:1. I knew that I had worked to the best of my ability under difficult circumstances, and I knew that I had gained enormously from this intellectual experience and would be satisfied with whatever came. My final thought was that exams were my last chance to show my worth, and I decided that there was nothing to lose by enjoying them and saying what I had to say, bearing in mind that I would need to back up my opinions. In the event the dreaded exams were almost fun. I said what I felt in my heart and I said why. For the first time ever I was confident in my opinion and reasoning and happy to stand by it, whether or not it was to the liking of my examiners. However, it seems that it was!

Having the Gall to Get a First in Biology
(Recollections and Advice from the Pre-Op)

Susan Anderton
First Class Honours in Biological Sciences
Lancaster University

Given the choice between an operation and taking my finals there really isn't any contest. The operation would get my vote each time. Unfortunately I was not given the luxury of a choice. My gall bladder developed a severe attitude problem during my third year and my operation to remove it was set for the day after my last exam - a novel way to celebrate finishing a degree! At least it gave me the opportunity to reflect over the course and contemplate whether a First was even a remote possibility.

I came late to higher education, after an Open University Science Foundation Course had whetted my appetite for study. I applied for a full-time place to study Biological Sciences at the ripe age of thirty-two. Somebody obviously agreed that this might be a good idea and offered me an unconditional place. Thus I began three years of hard work culminating, to my later surprise, in a First Class degree.

If I had known what a commitment it was going to be I might have thought harder about it. But, if all went dismally wrong, I could always return to my previous employment in the health sector. However, once I had discovered through my first pieces of work that I could achieve good marks, I was hooked. If I *was* going to do it then I was going to do it *well*. I think that is an important point. It is not worth starting a degree half-heartedly. You have to recognise that it is a commitment, it *will* butt into the social life sometimes, it *will* get frustrating, there *will* be tantrums and tears at times, but the end goal is worth it. No-one can *ever* take a First Class Honours degree away from you. And the fact is, with forward planning, organisation, good tactics and pig-headed perseverance anyone can set their sights on a First Class degree.

Before you start:

Consider carefully what type of degree you want to do and where. I was limited in my choice of university by my husband's work - moving house was not an option. Fortunately the local university had a modular course that was perfect for me. I could build up good marks from coursework alone and reduce the pressure during exams (which I hate nearly as much as spiders and housework). This is the first tactic - if you hate exams look for coursework-based courses, if you hate coursework look for exam-dominated courses. You know your own preferences so don't be pressed into applying for a course that you know won't suit you.

The lectures:

People have different ways of dealing with lectures. In the beginning I tried to get as much detail down as I could but this often left me with gaps to be filled in later. I finally discovered a way to make life a little easier. I invested in a small tape recorder and began taping my lectures. This also freed up time in the lectures to concentrate on diagrams, some of which were not available elsewhere. Free time was then spent rewriting the lectures. This was time-consuming but it meant that I had a good set of notes from which to work and revise in the future. The rewriting and re-reading also helped to settle facts in my mind, which helped later on in revision. I always tried to keep up to date with notes. There is little more challenging to your sanity than scattered, unfinished lecture notes just before exams start.

The practical sessions:

It is a fact that you get out of a course only what you put in. A little effort can reap bonuses in the future. Lecturers, I found, are more forthcoming if you show interest in their topics, particularly in practical sessions and tutorial groups (there's nothing worse than the embarrassed silence of a tutorial group struck dumb for an hour or more).

A mature attitude to practical sessions will be noticed and can only benefit you in the future. I found that enthusiasm often makes up for a lack of skill. For example, effort and interest put into mycological sketches from microscope slides resulted in good marks even though my artistic skills leave a little to be desired (actually they leave a *lot* to be desired).

The coursework:

Throughout my degree I concentrated on getting good coursework marks. Don't believe people who say, "You don't have to try in the first year because the results don't count towards your final class mark." The first year sets the scene for the following two years as lecturers assess your attitude and abilities. Effort can be repaid later since lecturers are often far more willing to spend time with you when you have a problem if they know that you are not a time-waster.

Presentation is important in obtaining good marks. Even though it was late at night and there was always something better to do (such as having a glass of wine or three), I always gave work a final read through after finishing. This prevented the unnecessary loss of marks for silly errors (my brain never functions well late at night, especially in the spelling department). I never got into the dangerous habit of relying on extensions for work either. These may be granted at a lecturer's discretion, but too many during the year will be noticed. Some lecturers may only give a 'pass' as the maximum grade for work handed in late - be warned!

I was very fortunate during my degree to find some very good friends. We tended to work together and support each other. This was a real blessing. We could borrow notes from each other if needed but, more importantly, we could talk to each other. As they say, three brain cells are better than one. Meetings over coffee often shed new light on topics and clarified points that we might have missed on our own. My degree owes much to my friends.

The exams:

On reflection these were the worst time for me. However, my efforts to accumulate marks during the year gave me a psychological advantage. The exams could only improve my overall grade.

Revision, as usual, was planned with the best intentions but often failed dismally. The best tip is self-discipline - to concentrate on the revision rather than the hundred-and-one other 'far more important things' that need doing at the time. I even cleaned and ironed, which, for me, is particularly sad.

At least by the time exams came round I knew I had a good set of notes to work from. I tended to write revision notes, a shortened version of each lecture, which could then be reduced to one A4 side as a memory-jogger.

I always tried to get several past exam papers to look at question-types and recurring topics. Timed completion of questions is a good way to begin pacing yourself for the actual exams. Some people argue that it is best to concentrate on just a few topics at the expense of others within a module. However, I have been caught out on this tactic and have faced a paper on which I recognised *nothing* that I had revised. I now try to cover all areas in a module but, looking at past papers and listening for hints from lecturers (they are often there somewhere), I concentrate more on areas that I feel confident with and less on the 'no-hope-of-ever-understanding' areas.

In the exams I usually read the paper first then sit with my eyes closed for a minute till I stop shaking. Then I re-read the paper. I try to take my time choosing which question to answer. The first instinct may not always provide the best question to do. Re-reading may shed new light on a question that, first time round, appeared impossible.

If, like me, you have problems during the exams, or during any other part of your course, talk to someone. The chances are that something can be done to help, or at least the circumstances can be taken into account when the examiners meet to award the final class of degree. It may not be easy but anything that relieves some of the pressure can only be of benefit to you. I informed all the relevant people and provided letters from my doctor to prove the fact. My knowing that the university knew and would take this into consideration if needed, helped me to cope with my finals. So it can be 'good to talk'.

After it's all finished you can relax and start the long wait for results. Or, if you want to be different like me, you can go into hospital and have your gall bladder removed (personally I would have preferred a bottle of wine!). But at least I went under the anaesthetic knowing that a First was possible, just like it can be for you or anyone else.

PS   *To prove that I am a serious biologist: I still have my gallstones in a jar for future research purposes!*

The Rest of My Life Depends on the Next Three Hours

Sheila Parnaby
First Class Honours in Occupational Therapy
The University College of Ripon and York St John

Final exams rank amongst the most anxiety-provoking times in a student's life. The whole three years seem to hinge on three short hours. I already had a job offer under my belt, but the fact that this was dependent upon gaining the qualification essential for State Registration was an added incentive. My complete professional career rested upon passing this exam. This kind of pressure, as anyone who has studied even basic psychology knows, can either provide motivation or totally destroy any chance of shining brightly as one would like.

Everyone has their own methods for coping and here are mine.

As a mature student, over forty years of age with a family, being prepared was my best weapon. For our final exams we were given broad topics and allowed to put together a folder with information gathered by ourselves to take into the exam. This was carefully assembled, cross-referenced and indexed. I had been warned, however, that this folder could be more of a distraction than helpful in a timed situation. I did not want to spend valuable time aimlessly flicking through the folder, risking not completing the questions.

I worked closely with three other students. The benefit of working together was to keep each other on track. I, in common with many who enjoy their subject, can produce ideas, and I think each one is pure genius. So, I had to be prepared to throw out the rubbish and develop the probable. This, for me, was only possible with the input and steadying influence of fellow students with whom I could work and trust. We examined the relationship between the previous year's topics and the actual questions set. We spent some time discussing and second-guessing what our questions could be. This strategy needs to be approached with caution and we knew this should only be used as a guide to preparation for the exam. Discovering you have gone off at a tangent and completely missed the point when faced with the exam paper is not to be recommended. The Occupational Therapy course is designed to prepare students to be competent basic grade OTs who understand their professional role within the work environment. So, as I understood it, this was what the final exam was testing us on. Having got this far through the course, the exam was not set to 'trip us up' but to give us a chance to finally prove we would be competent to practise - or so we were told.

The preparation began. Lecture notes and fieldwork experience were supplemented with information from journals, books and computer sources. Even the best university library won't have everything. One thing markers of exams like and which will get you those valuable extra points is 'showing wider reading' and 'evidence of learning beyond the course objectives'. So I did just that, by searching the computer-based indices and ordering copies of relevant articles or chapters from the British Library, which *does* have everything. I was lucky enough to live in York, close to the British Library at Boston Spa, and able to access up-to-date journals not available in the university. Time spent searching for extra information is always well spent.

Each of us in the 'swot' group researched different aspects or subjects and pooled the information. The next stage of the process took determination and dedication. Using the possible essay titles from our second-guessing stage I wrote sample essays. Only two of us in the 'swot' group managed this stage. With a couple of weeks to go before exams, continuing to gather information seemed preferable to writing essays. However enticing that option seemed at the time, I knew that during the exam I would have regretted not following the plan through.

Writing the sample essays was extremely hard. It took much longer than the time allocated in an exam, but I had that luxury. The essays I produced were adequate, but unlikely to set the world alight. Time for consultation again. We read each other's efforts and pointed out what had been missed, taking out irrelevancies, expanding on points. This was valuable to all in the group, whether we wrote sample essays or not. Our experience of lecturers' styles gave us some idea of what approach received the higher marks. The time spent on the essays allowed us to bring in lucid arguments relevant to the topics, checking we had a balance and integrating the information we had gathered. Through the discussions we felt that we had developed that all important 'critical personal engagement' so loved by examiners. This did mean that our essays shared some details and information, but we kept to our own styles and in the end we each answered different questions.

With all of this done, knowing everything that I had prepared in the best way possible, I allowed myself some time off before the exam and, in theory at least, was rested and ready for the day.

Time was ticking away and by the time the exam came I had in my folder relevant, and I have to admit, much irrelevant information, plus the sample essays. Not unexpectedly the questions were not exactly as predicted, but they were close enough to adapt the introductions and pull out opinions backed up with balanced arguments that were relevant to the questions. With the preparation described, my mind was clear enough to focus on answering questions. I didn't have to hold the jumble of ideas in my head, or, worse, panic about going completely blank.

For exams where you are unable to take in a folder which, granted, is most of them, practising essays is still an excellent way to prepare. Time spent writing, working on and improving essays then condensing them down to key words, makes remembering much easier. Even if you can't remember it all, you will write a better essay than you would have done without the preparation.

More and more courses base results on assignments but still have an exam somewhere. Look at exams as an opportunity to show what you *do* know. Examiners look for thoroughness, consistency and attention to detail, but mark more leniently than they would an assignment. Preparation will reduce the panic and stress and leave you more able to display your knowledge on the day.

Did the rest of my life really depend on a three-hour exam, or on what I did in those weeks leading up to it? The Occupational Therapy course was designed to encourage working together, sharing ideas and skills, and I used that to my advantage. But probably the most important factor in achieving academic success was that I *enjoyed* studying for a profession in which I believe. I never lost sight of my goal of qualifying as an occupational therapist and this, to me, was, and still is, more important than the degree itself. And it was that that kept me focused throughout my studies. I prepared for my exams whilst working part-time and looking after my two school-aged children. There is no magical solution, and I am no genius. Being organised was the key and it is not, for me, a natural talent, but a skill acquired out of necessity. I am now looking forward to starting work as a fully-qualified OT. So, something that seemed to me to be impossible a few years ago has at last become a reality.

From the Factory Floor...
an interview with

Marc Dellerba
First Class Honours in Chemical Sciences
Lancaster University

Why, in a nutshell, do you think you got a First?

The amount of work I put in in the first and second year really.

The first and second year in particular? Why's that?

The actual structure of the course. There's an awful lot that's carried through. I mean you get a lot of foundation in the first year, a lot of basics. And I really learnt all of that so it set me up quite well for the second year that was actually the hardest year. It was near enough double the workload compared to the third year. You did exams straight after Easter. Then you got a further set of modules and you got examined on them again at the end of the summer term. And by the end of that I'd really had enough.

But having that good base from the first year helped. Then you know that if something has gone in once when you return to it it's more just to refresh your mind.

Obviously you did get a First at the end of the day so what else would you say you did right?

In the second year and the third year it's really important not only to get the modules you want, but also the lecturers who you know can teach you. I mean I ended up doing stuff that wouldn't have been my first choice but I did it because of the actual lecturers. I knew that at the end of the day, even if it was a subject I found quite difficult, these people could put it across to me.

Having said that it's not like you can base your whole degree on them, because it's an accredited degree for the RSC - Royal Society of Chemistry. So they lay down the minimum modular core which you have to take to get RSC recognition. You don't really get a great deal of freedom.

Why did you do chemistry?

I just found I could do it. I did chemistry, biology and physics and I realised I was no mathematician pretty instantly. Biology was all right but I just really got into organic chemistry.

So would you have specific advice for chemistry undergraduates who are wanting to get a First?

Um, I don't know.... I think you've really got to enjoy your subject. If you don't really, really enjoy it then, you know, it's going to be three years of really hard work. You have to have that initial interest or you're just going to weigh yourself down. You've got to get to know your lecturers too. At the end of the day they're really into that subject as well and they're very open to you going and seeing them. And if you're dead straight with them then you can learn a lot that way. I don't think I would even have got a degree without the support I got from all the lecturers ....

The revision thing's really important.

Have you got a technique for that?

I haven't got a revision technique as such. One thing I did do in the first year was to spend an awful lot of time revising the stuff I wasn't particularly strong at - assuming that I'm an absolute genius at the stuff I thought I *was* good at and that it would carry me through, which was a load of rubbish. So I ended up doing quite well in physical chemistry and not particularly well in stuff I thought I could do. It's really important to revise everything.

Then I've spent hours and hours going over the last five years' papers looking for patterns and you know you can figure that out. But that really fell down for me in the first year.

So the only strategy I *have* used is to make sure I concentrate on what I am good at. The way the marks are put together those high seventy, eighty percents can pull your weaker subjects up a bit.

There were big chunks of modules I didn't understand and never really got to grips with. You tend to do stuff like do a bit of memorising so you can actually regurgitate something on paper. Even though you don't understand it you can still put down the equation.

That's something you can do in the sciences but you can't do that so much in arts subjects. You learn the facts but the facts are only a skeleton if you like. You still have to build an argument.

Hmm... You get questions where they're just asking for - 'work out the value of this reaction' - and you don't have to understand the value, you don't have to understand particularly the assumptions behind the way the equation's set out, you don't have to particularly understand what each individual part means, and it's very... you know, you can just copy basically - a repetition kind of thing. You've seen it done, you do it once, and then repeat it.

What about your family and friends, how did they react to you getting a First?

Oh, really pleased. I mean I'm the only one in our family ever to have got past sixth form I think. Nobody's ever gone to university.

I've got no academic background as such you see. I came off the factory floor, went through this Open College thing.... I think I've got a low grade CSE in chemistry from when I was at school. So I didn't actually know an awful lot about the subject.

So would you say there *is* anything in your background that has helped or hindered in any sense?

Well it did help coming from the factory floor. I mean I'd been working for two years and the thought of getting away from that... It was a little extra push. That's the only thing really. Knowing that I don't want to sit there and watch a machine for the rest of my life.

What about life skills that you've acquired?

I've no reservations about going up and actually talking to a lecturer as another person, which I think with the younger students can be a bit of a problem. I'm pretty sure that some people manage to never speak to a lecturer in the whole of the three years.

What's the point of getting a First?

I don't know... well, I do know. The personal satisfaction at the end of the day. To have actually really worked, particularly in the second year when it was hell at times..... well, I would have been a bit miffed not to have got that First at the end of the day.

Were there times when you thought you might not get a First?

Yeah, well, before the exams I was quite happy because I knew all I had to get was sixty percent and I'd be all right. But, when I came out to see who was being viva'd... You see I'd assumed everyone who got a First would be viva'd. And my name wasn't up there. Before I started university the thought of getting a 2:1 was just a dream.. But then I started getting these marks and, well, when I actually thought I was going to *get* a 2:1... I wasn't particularly nice to be with that evening.

Could anyone get a First?

I've talked this over with other people and I'm of the opinion that if I can get a First, yeah, anybody can get a First, because I think a lot of it is hard work.

Would you do it again?

Yeah. You can't go back. You could find me on the shop floor now and ask me whether I'd do it and, yes, I'd do it again.

First Class Students are Ordinary People

Stuart J Brinkworth
First Class Honours in Law
Lancaster University

Extraordinary people are ordinary people with extraordinary determination

Introduction

It is probably true to say that for most students the attainment of a First Class degree in any discipline is perceived as something which is achieved by someone other than themselves. In other words, only extraordinary people - those from a certain social background and with a certain education - have the necessary capabilities to achieve such a grade. Being someone who considers himself to be as ordinary as the next student, which was certainly my view, at least during the early stages of my degree.

However, such perceptions are very much misconceived. Believe it or not a First Class degree could be within the grasp of the vast majority of students, many of whom realise too late to fulfil their true potential. That is because to become an extraordinary, or First Class, student, has little to do with social background and prior education, and everything to do with one's attitude towards not only one's studies, but oneself. This state of mind, the magic formula that worked so well for me, is quite simply that of *determination*.

This may well sound easy enough, after all most students are determined to do well during their degrees. But being determined to do well and having the determination that is required to obtain a First Class degree is not one and the same thing - the two are virtually poles apart. Indeed, what really surprised me during my studies was that there were very few students who either knew what it took or had what it took to succeed.

The quality that they lacked was what I call *extraordinary determination*. For me this can be divided into two independent but interrelated elements, viz., *motivation* and *commitment*. It is the combination of both these elements which is really the key to success at any level of life, not just in academic studies. There is little point in being motivated if one cannot give 100% commitment, and one cannot give 100% commitment if one isn't motivated.

What follows below, then, is an exposition of how ordinary people can attain a First Class degree, and what the two elements of extraordinary determination mean in practice, based very much on my own experience.

Motivation

This is the crux of attaining a First Class degree, for motivation is really the fuel that powers the engine of determination. However, motivation is an extremely personal and individual force because what motivates each and every one of us has to do with our own personal experiences as well as our future aspirations.

This was particularly true in the case of my own motivations. My background was slightly different to most since I entered university as a mature student at the age of 25. For almost 6 years prior to starting my degree I worked as a Health Inspector in local government. During that time I had become increasingly frustrated at the lack of opportunities my career was providing. My instincts told me that I had to strike out and strive to find a more intellectually profitable path. This quest for personal satisfaction was also heightened by my determination to prove myself to my old work colleagues, many of who had doubted my ability to finish my degree, let alone achieve a First.

Moreover, there was a massive part of me that wanted to exorcise the ghosts of my comprehensive school education. This particular period of my life had seen me waste my very capable brain by exuding little effort or enthusiasm towards my studies, much to the frustration of teachers and family alike. It was probably this, more than anything else, which drove me onward. I felt the need to prove to myself that I could achieve what I always thought I was capable of, and I was not prepared to make the same mistakes again.

Every student who aspires to achieve a First Class degree must ask why they want to achieve it. This may not seem important, but the answer can make all the difference to the outcome. In my experience, those students who are motivated purely by the supposed financial rewards that a First can bring, rarely achieve their goal of attaining it. This is because the motivation required to propel you along must be of a much deeper and more meaningful type. To achieve a First one has to be fully embraced by the topic that is being studied. This requires a real and deeper interest in the topic, one that extends way beyond where it can lead in materialistic terms. This was a fact overlooked by many students I knew, all of whom produced rather soulless 2:1s instead of heartfelt Firsts.

Commitment

If motivation is the fuel that drives the engine of determination, then commitment is the oil that keeps that engine running smoothly. In fact this is where the major problem arises for the vast majority of students, even those who are very well motivated. A degree means many things to many people but, for most, the time spent at university is just as much a social as an academic learning curve. Thus, more often than not, the ambitious student will be caught in the dilemma between wanting to enjoy him or herself, and wanting to obtain a First Class degree.

The truth of the matter is, a First Class degree is not a beer drinker's degree. This is because the golden rule of commitment is the unwavering prioritisation of one's lifestyle. In other words, study becomes the number one priority.

However, please don't be mistaken into thinking that this means continuous study 24 hours a day, 7 days a week, because it does not. What it does mean is that if you want to get everything you hoped for from university, namely a First Class degree while having a life, then you must organise your time in such a way as to achieve both objectives. This means the maximisation of all available time, including getting out of bed early in the morning. As unbelievable as it sounds, the hours prior to midday do exist. Indeed, it really is amazing how much time in the evening can be freed up by getting out of bed and studying early. I made sure that I was in the library by 9 am most days, and never left much before 7 pm, quite often later. And, where all else failed, I found the ability to stay awake for extended periods during the early hours invaluable.

Whilst this may all sound quite benign, the harsh reality is that it is not. In fact it is extremely tough. There were times when I turned up to lectures, seminars, and even football matches absolutely exhausted because I had stayed up all night catching up with my reading. There were also times when I felt that I couldn't cope with the pressure I was placing myself under. It is at these times that you feel most like settling for a 2:1, and it is also at these times that you find out whether you have the commitment that is required to go all the way.

There is no simple solution to this problem when it arises. For me something had to give. I chose to stop playing football during the most strenuous times, although I never quite managed to stop drinking and always seemed to make it to the bar even if it was only for last orders. Ultimately, of course, this proves one thing: commitment will invariably mean sacrifice, and it is at this point that prioritisation is vitally important.

In saying all that, when it comes down to it, the practicalities of attaining a First Class degree depend on the ability to gain First Class marks in exams and, in the case of most universities these days, essays.

As far as essays are concerned the essential prerequisite is depth and breadth of research, and that means commitment to reading. My success over others stemmed from the fact that I was prepared to spend hours reading around the topics that I was writing about, exploring avenues that others had neither the time nor the inclination to pursue. This enabled me to come up with original ideas and produce thorough, watertight arguments.

In contrast, the perceived lottery of exams produces a different type of challenge to the First Class student, since much seems to depend on how you perform on the day. In saying that, it may surprise you to know that exams are essentially 90% perspiration and 10% inspiration. Preparation is everything. By keeping on top of my reading throughout the year, I gained an advantage over other students when it came to revising. Whilst they were using up much of their early revision time reading texts that they should have read months previously, I was busy condensing and organising my notes.

Notwithstanding this, for me the most important aspect of preparation is exam technique. In my experience, a good examination answer is one that is prepared outside of the examination hall and imported for use during the exam. Thus I spent hours practising timed essays, anticipating questions and writing and learning model answers. By the time it came to each exam, I merely had to recall the particular model answer I had prepared, or adapt those which did not quite fit.

And finally .....

Perhaps the most important point to remember is that a First Class degree lies at the end of a very long road, one which has many hills and mountains to be climbed before it can be reached. What I have attempted to show here is not only that the vehicle best equipped for such a journey is that of extraordinary determination, but what exactly the characteristics of that vehicle are. In other words, what is required to turn oneself from an ordinary student into a First Class student.

In the end, no matter how intelligent the student, there is really no way of avoiding the essential aspect of gaining a First Class degree - hard work. Of course, just as intelligence alone is no guarantee of attaining a First, neither is hard work. It is simply that one stands more chance with the latter than the former.

The 'Ah' Factor:
How to Succeed in Computer Science

Gary Rigg
First Class Honours in Computer Science with Software
Engineering
Lancaster University

It's always a difficult question to answer when people ask me, "So, how exactly did you get a First?" because I don't really know. Getting a First isn't always planned. Sometimes it just happens. I certainly didn't work myself into the ground day in and day out. In fact, with regard to effort, I believe I only just earned myself a Second Class degree. This leaves me with only one conclusion: my technique must have been right. And that's what I'm going to discuss here.

I guess the first correct move I made was my choice of subject. I've always had an interest in computers from a hobby perspective, although, to be honest, prior to university, this only stretched as far as using the computer as a source of entertainment - just how far could I get in 'Doom' without cheating? However, I do think that if you get the chance to study a hobby then you should do it. That way half the battle is already won and you are open to the *'ah' factor*. I lost count of the number of times I sat in a lecture (or, to be more honest, sat in my room revising previously unseen course notes for a set of lectures I apparently attended) and something would just click. I'd think to myself, "Ah yes, so that's how that's done" or "Ah, that's why that happens". Put simply, I was learning something that related directly back to my hobby, and when you learn something that way you don't forget. Even if you're already into your degree, try and pick options which appeal to you, hobbies or not. Remember, this isn't school anymore, you're supposed to get something out of the course as well!

If you're studying computer science it's more than likely the case that you'll have to do a final year project. At Lancaster University I was informed that the project often dictated your overall result. People rarely got a degree classification a grade or higher than that awarded for their project. With this in mind pick an interesting topic, something guaranteed to give you enthusiasm. Ignore the suggested topics if they don't appeal. Do what you want. It's important, however, that when you use this approach you choose something suitably difficult and adventurous as well as interesting. Then you're bound to succeed. The 'ah' factor alone will drive you to work at it while the fact that the project's aims exceed the norm will win most examiners over, even if you don't achieve what you set out to do.

A sound revision strategy is what you'll need next. It's a misconception that achieving a First requires working from dusk till dawn. A lot of it's about how effective your revision is. First of all, work to a timetable. Set out what you need to do and when. Make absolutely sure you have a balance of everything. Spend time on all your subjects - guessing your way into an exam doesn't work. Be prepared to answer a question on anything. Then, if your approach is good, you should have plenty of time to spare for social activities and other hobbies. Besides which, it's easy to fall into a revision trap. When you revise too much you hit a point where no amount of further revision will do you any good. You simply can't absorb any more. And the same can happen if you revise for long periods without a break. You end up revising but not learning and the whole process becomes depressing and counter-productive. I also recommend that you work on the basis of startlines and not deadlines. Decide when you're going to *start* revising a certain topic. It's all too easy to push a deadline back and neglect work but to change a startline requires restarting your revision timetable. This may sound like I'm playing with words but it does work. You'll automatically meet the deadlines simply because you have startlines to meet. Just make sure that your startlines aren't unrealistic. So, that's the planning out of the way - a scheduled balance of work and play. All that remains is the revision itself. What's the best way to do this? You guessed it: it's the 'ah' factor all over again.

I always approached revision by performing a number of passes over the material. Firstly, I'd read the material ensuring that I understood it, making the connections and seeing how the topics were interrelated. In a nutshell, I'd attempt to grasp the overall picture. This understanding is the key and implicitly involves the 'ah' factor. Go over your notes thoroughly, highlighter in hand and ensure you understand the material. Don't revise one topic and then leave it for a long period of time - everything will be gone. Go over a revised topic quickly a day or so later to help it gel in your mind.

It's nigh on impossible to remember all the details of all the subjects you'll be examined on. Quite often you know the material but you can't quite recall it (it's a bit like having a word on the tip of your tongue!). The best way around this is to work on the idea of a trigger. You can use a trigger to prompt your mind. You bring on the 'ah' factor yourself. As an example, make your own acronyms or short stories revolving around a topic. Even write a song if it helps. Obviously you have to traverse your knowledge when learning in this way (for example, you couldn't tell someone what line six of a song was without singing it through) but that's a small price to pay for the amount of knowledge you'll be able to store.

My final piece of advice revolves around last minute revision. I've been told a number of times in the past that "If you don't know it now you never will". I'm sure you've heard the expression. What a load of tripe! From my experience last minute revision can be the most effective, even on the morning of the exam, if it's prepared for and done correctly. When you're reaching the end of your revision and you're revising topics for the last time, write the key points and methods down separately along with all the triggers you've derived. You should aim to have a full course summarised on a few sheets of paper. This is extremely useful because when you do your last minute revision you only need to read over your final summary. Read it as often as time will allow, you'll only have a little to learn and remembering it shouldn't be too difficult. Then, when you're in the exam and answering a question, scribble all the related key points and triggers you can remember down in pencil. Cue the 'ah' factor and each point should hopefully cause a chain reaction of triggers - remembering one detail leads to another and so on, enabling you to recall pages of the material you revised. Not bad when all you actually learnt properly was a few bullet points!

I guess that's basically it. I would suggest practising these methods before using them, just to make sure they're right for you. But, the next time someone asks you for a useful strategy for obtaining a First, start by telling them, "Ah, I remember.....".

Passing the First Threshold

Paul Sutherland
First Class Honours in English
The University College of Ripon and York St John

I graduated from the University College of Ripon and York St John's at the age of fifty. In Canada, thirty-five years before, I had retreated from the boisterous energy of teenage friends - when playing street-football - into the stillness of the attic to write poetry. This withdrawal signalled a sudden intellectual intent. Yet, at twenty-one, I dropped out of a Canadian university after an adventurous but undisciplined year. It was the late 1960s. I had spent my academic time in a newly-equipped record library listening to the *Jimi Hendrix Experience*, the *Doors* and *Cream*. This missed opportunity resulted in twenty-five years of indecision.

9:30ish, October 1994 - the first English class at St John's: "Reading Text". The room rustled with inattention. Every student seemed to possess a piece of paper: not the course outline, but letters, invitations, postcards and notices for a dance, a film or a party. I exaggerate: the young were justly absorbed in the sensation of being free and away from home. I had sat in a similar lecture room before, and misread the signs. The note paper, book pages, and tall windows had inferred to me permissiveness and freedom, when they had really meant study, involvement and academic rigour - a paradox of: 'have a good time and if need be earn money', but do the assignment work. Even then I did not accept the strength of this message until I received a limping B- for an initial essay. I had tried to construct my argument during a weekend wedged in between visits from friends. It was not, and would never be, enough preparation. Education, I realised, did not represent a pastime, but a diligent entrenchment, digging in and giving each subject the hours.

Reinforced by a few indifferent early results, an alarm bell struck in me 'not again'. At the same time, from an opposite perspective, a tantony sounded, gradually growing in percussion - a friend saying "You'll have to get a First" and my girlfriend's refrain "You can do it". In the lagging middle of my final exam in the third year, her phrase, like the ting of a glass bowl being struck once, resonated in my thoughts. In achieving a First the encouragement of others was of great value.

My first year's struggle was turning comments on my essays from "Promising" into "Excellent". I realised a need for stamina and focused, critical thinking, for breadth and depth. No weekend dashes. Two weeks for most two thousand word assignments. Tutors reacted generously to my enthusiasm, as did younger students. In a module, "Communication Skills", eighteen and nineteen year olds respected my willingness to 'stick my neck out' and ask questions. Discussion stimulated group involvement, making sessions more animated and engaging (as the tutor remarked in his course review). In the long run, constructive relations with tutors through active participation, and with students through sharing in their intellectual struggles, enhanced my three years at college.

Balancing openness with fear of plagiarism was another problem. Hoarding of knowledge, when students control information in fear of someone else using the material, is a threat to academia. As an undergraduate, if a student discussed a specific novel or play with me, I responded openly, convinced that in my essays, or in an exam, a cosmos of data would yet remain to be explored. Defensiveness deters scholarship and it appears this collaborative attitude has served my aspirations. At my Canadian university, only entering into dialogue with a few tutors, and avoiding studious undergraduates, I had left after a year. At St John's, readily conversing with students and members of staff, I earned a First.

In my second year I accepted a new challenge. Knowing the English Faculty would welcome the creation of an in-house, student-inspired magazine I undertook producing one as an Independent Learning Unit. An ILU is assessed like any course and contains an equivalent workload. Creating the magazine called *DreamCatcher* brought me into closer liaison with my personal tutor, a senior lecturer. Through publicising, collecting submissions, editing, and production, I changed from an isolated student into a member of an academic institution. This extent of participation was disconcerting. Instead of using avoidance tactics, as in my first encounter with higher education, I produced a work that potentially every tutor and student on the campuses of York and Ripon could examine and metaphorically grade. This was an overt test of my intellect. The success of *DreamCatcher*, after two issues, has led the Faculty to commit itself to future publications. The finished magazine's impact on my degree award is hard to estimate, yet its qualitative influence was enormous.

In pursuing a First the end of my second year was vital. Each student needed to choose their final year subjects and select a research topic for their ten thousand word Special Study (dissertation). Timetable allowing, I chose subjects in which I had proven capability and interest. As the topic for my Study I elected T S Eliot, a poet I had often read and whose work was topical due to Anthony Julius' *T S Eliot, anti-Semitism and literary form*. This gave rise to cross-references between my dissertation and coursework in my main area of modernism. From my last six courses, five were related to modernist issues. For me - relating to subject choice - the first year had presented a chance for experimenting. But by the second I was circumspect; by the third, determined.

Against this concentration, I notice a counter-trend from my year as a fresher. In early bibliographies I listed between five and ten authors. In the second year works referred to grew from fifteen to twenty, and in the third, twenty to twenty-five or more, though assignment lengths stayed relatively consistent. My reading-speed had dramatically increased. Also I drew from wide ranging sources, not only classic literary criticisms, but recent publications, newspaper articles, and journals, using CD-ROM facilities, but always closely reading the text and taking extensive notes.

Achieving a First was not winning a game but the consequence of diligence, observable through the expansion of research. I had learned to adapt to changing circumstances. The transition from second to third year can be traumatic and deceptive. The amount of work does not radically increase, but a greater level of discernment is demanded. Also, though communiqués from the registrar suggest the second year's grades count, students tend to believe results of the final year determine their degree. My experiences confirm this assumption. Significantly, I found productive ways to react to the greater pressure and altering requirements. This included reading books from the 'Modernism' list, during the summer.

Based on this optimism I should have strolled through my leaving year. And after a time, lecturers hinted "You have nothing to worry about". But my last months at college were complicated by intense uncertainty. In retrospect, the years of indecision sprung a final backlash against my new-recovered confidence and self-respect. I was surly and irritable. Tutors noted my downcast appearance. In those weeks before the 'finals' I was one more undergraduate striving towards an elusive goal. The approaching exams represented a powerful equaliser that all students had to negotiate. For us, the fear of the world beyond education produced distress, but also the knowledge (and evidence) that in the final stretch one could trip, stumble or fall. Sitting on Graduation Day in the nave of the York Minster those insecurities were disarmingly remote. The task completed, the opportunity not lost, I thought, I had gained such a coign of vantage of the structure's interior, elegantly lit, at that moment the apposite to my success and joy.

Looking back, my equivocal quarter-century was not wasted. The many jobs and concerted reading undertaken during that time provided a reservoir of knowledge and experience on which I could draw. In the middle of those former years, employed as a cleaner with no prospects, I habitually stopped on a particular bridge and, gazing up-river, reaffirmed my faith in my intelligence. And occasionally at college I would withdraw to a side-chapel to reflect on the immediate purpose: the obtaining of a university education. It was not my ambition to gain a First, but to do as well as I could.

At university students confront intense and contradictory feelings: from the boot-camp atmosphere of Induction Week, to the sudden dispersal after the finals, with undergraduates departing towards every compass point. Possibly, I obtained a First because I was slightly distant from emotional fluctuations, neither aloof nor enacting the socialite role. Nevertheless, there are friendships I would like to retain, with co-graduates and tutors who recognise, perhaps better than me, the depth and grit involved in achieving a First Class Honours degree.

Other titles in the IHE Series:

They always eat green apples: *images of university and decisions at 16*
Mike Heathfield and Nine Wakeford
ISBN: 0 901800 16 3   Type: Paperback   Price: £6.95

Juggling for a degree: *mature students' experience of university life*
Edited by Hilary Arksey, Ian Marchant and Cheryl Simmill
ISBN: 0 901800 49 X   Type: Paperback   Price: £6.95

How's your dissertation going: *students share the rough reality of dissertation and project work*
Liz Hampson
ISBN: 0 901800 51 1   Type: Paperback   Price: £6.95

In at the deep end: *first experiences of university teaching*
Edited by David Allan
ISBN: 0 901800 90 2   Type: Paperback   Price: £7.95

It's quite an education: *supporting your son or daughter through university*
Edited by Lynne Boundy
ISBN: 0 901800 98 8   Type: Paperback   Price: £7.95

Beg, borrow or starve?: *how to finance your degree*
Anthony Hesketh
ISBN: 0 901800 99 6   Type: Paperback   Price: £7.95

Uneasy Chairs: *life as a professor*
Edited by Jeffrey Richards
ISBN: 1-86220-042-4   Type: Paperback   Price: £7.95

Take a Minute: *reflections on modern higher education administration*
Edited by Helena Thorley
ISBN: 1-86220-043-2   Type: Paperback   Price: £7.95

48 Warm-ups for group work
Edited by Jo Malseed
Type: Spiral bound   Price: £4.95

Also available through IHE:

Health Promoting Universities: *concept, experience and framework for action*
Edited by Ágis D Tsouros, Gina Dowding, Jane Thompson, Mark Dooris
Published by World Health Organisation
ISBN 92 890 1285 4   Type: Paperback   Price: £20

For further information or to order any of the above titles please contact: Mrs Linda Cook, Unit for Innovation in Higher Education, Lonsdale College, Lancaster University, Lancaster LA1 4YN.
Tel: 01524 592137   Fax: 01524 843934
Email: l.cook@lancaster.ac.uk